Tagalog Structures

PALI LANGUAGE TEXTS: PHILIPPINES

Social Sciences and Linguistics Institute
University of Hawaii

Howard P. McKaughan
Editor

TAGALOG
STRUCTURES

TERESITA V. RAMOS

University of Hawaii Press
Honolulu

The work reported herein was performed pursuant to a contract with the Peace Corps, Washington, D.C. 20525. The opinions expressed herein are those of the author and should not be construed as representing the opinions or policies of any agency of the United States government.

University of Hawai'i Press books are printed on acid-free paper and meet the guidelines for permanence and durability of the Council on Library Resources

PREFACE

This synopsis has the purpose of assisting the learner of Tagalog understand basic structures. In order to learn the language, the structures must be internalized. An understanding of major structures will help in the internalization process.

These materials are a part of a series of instructional materials developed for major Philippine languages under a Peace Corps Contract (PC25-1507) through the Pacific and Asian Linguistics Institute at the University of Hawaii. Other materials on Tagalog include <u>Tagalog for Beginners</u> by Teresita V. Ramos and Videa de Guzman and <u>Tagalog Dictionary</u> by Miss Ramos.

It is the hope of the editor of the series and the author of this synopsis that these materials will encourage further grammatical studies as well as the learning of Tagalog.

Howard P. McKaughan
Editor

CONTENTS

x

TAGALOG STRUCTURES

I. PHONOLOGY

Tagalog has 16 consonant sounds, 5 vowel sounds and 6 diphthongs. Syllables are either stressed (´) or unstressed (unmarked). It further has three terminal junctures: level, a slight fall and a slight rise. Finally, it has three pitches: low, level, and rising.

1. Consonants

The Tagalog consonants are b, d, k, g, h, l, m, n, ng, p, ', r, s, t, w, y. Ng represents the velar nasal and ' represents the glottal stop. The following chart shows the articulatory descriptions of each of the consonants.

Consonant Chart

		Labial	Dental	Palatal	Velar	Glottal
Stops	Vl. Vd.	p b	t d		k g	'
Fricatives	Vl.		s			h
Nasals	Vd.	m	n		ng	
Laterals	Vd.		l			
Flap	Vd.		r			
Semi-Vowel	Vd.	w		y		

The glottal stop '

The glottal stop may cause an English speaker some difficulties because it is not significant in his system; i.e., it does not make a difference in meaning. In Tagalog, however, the absence or the presence of the glottal stop as the final sound of a word may result in a difference in meaning. Note the following examples.

báta 'bathrobe, nightgown' bata' 'child'

bága 'live coal'   baga' 'lung'

The glottal stop ' is produced when the glottis or the opening between the vocal cords is tightly closed, stopping the air coming from the lungs. In Tagalog it always occurs before a word written with an initial vowel, or between two vowels written adjacent to each other. If it occurs in word final position, it is marked by the apostrophe (') in this text.

In rapid speech, the final glottal stop within phrases or sentences may disappear. Note the following:

(Basá') Basa siya kanina.
         'He was wet a while ago.'

(Pasá') May pasa siya.
         'He has a bruise.'

The consonant ng

The velar nasal (ng) is difficult for an English speaker to produce when it occurs in word or syllable initial position because it never occurs in this position in English. Examples in initial word and syllable position follow:

ngayón	now
ngití'	smile
ngánga'	mixture of betel nut leaf and lime for chewing
ngawá'	to cry, howl
ngípin	tooth
ngitngít	irritation
ngatngát	to gnaw
ngúnit	but
nguyá'	to chew
ngiwí'	to be distorted, twisted

Generally, n̲ is substituted for n̲g̲ by American learners of Tagalog when the latter occurs in the syllable initial position. The following examples show the two sounds at the beginning of words having different meanings:

nawá'	may it be so	ngawá'	to cry, howl
naknák	an abscess	ngakngák	to cry aloud
nána'	pus	ngánga'	betel nut mixture for chewing

The initial voiceless stops p, t, k

Tagalog p̲, t̲, and k̲ in word initial position are not aspirated (pronounced with a puff of air). English p̲, t̲, and k̲ however are aspirated. The English speaker of Tagalog therefore tends to aspirate these sounds. Aspirated p̲, t̲, and k̲ do not change the meaning of Tagalog words but if used they give the speaker a foreign accent. Examples of the p̲, t̲, and k̲ in initial position follow:

p̲	t̲	k̲
pitó	tíra	kúlay
payát	tubó	kaniyá
pángit	tapón	kílay
paták	túbig	kánan
pagpág	totoó	kasí

The p̲, t̲, and k̲ unaspirated sounds in spark, steam, and scream approximate the pronunciation of the Tagalog p̲, t̲, and k̲.

The consonant r

The r̲ in English is retroflexed, that is the tongue is curled back into the area of the palate. It does not touch the roof of the mouth. The Tagalog r̲ however is produced with the tongue tapping the gum ridge quickly as happens for the t̲t̲ in Betty for some. Again as with p̲, t̲, and k̲, pronouncing the English r̲ in place of the Tagalog r̲ would not change the meaning of words, but it would affect the clarity of communication.

The consonant 1

Like r, the difference between the Tagalog 1 and
English 1 is in the production of the sound. The
English 1 is produced with the tongue tip at some point
along the roof of the mouth, leaving the sides of the
tongue open for the air to flow out. The Tagalog 1 on
the other hand has the tongue flat from the tip to the
back, with the tip back of the upper teeth. Examples
of words with 1 are the following:

Initial	Medial	Final
lápit	alás	baól
láson	alám	búrol
láyon	balík	salawál
lángit	bálot	kapál

The consonant d

The consonant d often becomes r in intervocalic
positions. For example:

d	r
daan	apat na raan
gayon din	gaya rin
kudkud	kudkuran

Exceptions to this rule are in borrowed words like
rádyo 'radio' and reló 'watch, clock'.

Consonants t, d, n, and s

Tagalog t, d, n, and s are pronounced with the
tongue tip at the back of the upper teeth. English t,
d, n, and s are produced with the tongue tip behind the
upper gum ridge. These sounds pronounced as alveolars
rather than as dentals do not change the meaning of
Tagalog words but do produce some confusion in communication.

The rest of the Tagalog consonant sounds h, b, g,
m, y, and w do not cause much difficulty for the speaker
of English because they are fairly similar to the

corresponding sounds in English.

2. Vowels

   Tagalog vowels are i, e, a, o, and u. The vowel
chart below shows roughly the tongue height and its
fronting or backing in the mouth when each of the vowel
sounds is produced.

Vowel Chart

	Front	Central	Back
High	i		u
Mid	e		o
Low		a	

   The vowel o varies freely with u and so does e with
i. They are considered separate sounds from u and i
because in a few examples they distinguish meaning.
The mid vowels e and o are fairly new sounds assimilated
in the language from Spanish. Examples of the u/o and
i/e contrasts are as follows:

e vs. i

mésa	table	mísa	mass
téla	cloth	tíla	maybe
bénta	sale	bínta	moro canoe

o vs. u

óso	bear	úso	fad

3. Diphthongs

   Tagalog diphthongs are iw, ey, ay, aw, oy and uy.
Diphthongs are complex sounds which are combinations of
simple vowel sounds and semi-vowels.

Diphthong Chart

	Front	Central	Back
High	iw		uy
Mid	ey		oy
Low		ay aw	

Except for iw and uy all the Tagalog diphthongs
have their corresponding sounds in English. The diphthong iw may cause problems in production because
speakers of English tend to break the diphthong into two
syllables. Thus sísiw, 'chick' may become [sísiyew],
incorrect for Tagalog.

Some words with the iw and uy diphthongs are the
following:

iw	uy
iwan	uy
iwi	aruy
giliw	kasuy
bitiw	tsapsuy
aliw	tsampuy

4. Consonant Clusters

Originally Tagalog did not have initial or final
consonant clusters. The medial clusters were and still
are usually found across syllable boundaries. Due to
assimilated borrowed words (mostly Spanish), there are
now Tagalog initial consonant clusters. Only s, l, r,
w, and y can occur as the second consonant. With s,
only t can occur as the first consonant:

tsinélas	slippers
tsaá	tea
tsápa	badge
tsíp	chief

```
        tsámba                  luck

        tsampurádo              porridge
```

The following list gives examples of what initial consonants can co-occur with r, l, w, and y to form the clusters:

	-r	-l	-w	-y
p-	prito 'fried'	plato 'plate'	pwede 'ok'	pyano 'piano'
t-	trapo 'rag'		twalya 'towel'	tya 'aunt'
k-	krema 'cream'	klase 'class'	kwarta 'money'	kyosko 'kiosk'
b-	braso 'arm'	blusa 'blouse'	bwaya 'crocodile'	byuda 'widow'
d-	drama 'drama'		dwende 'dwarf'	dyan 'there'
g-	gripo 'faucet'	glorya 'glory'	gwantes 'glove'	
(f-)		Flóra 'Flora'		
s-			swéldo 'salary'	syá 'she'
h-			hwág 'don't'	hyá' 'shame'
n-			nwéstra 'Our Lady'	nyán 'of that'
m-			mwélye 'pier'	myámya' 'by and by'

A few final clusters occur in Tagalog:

-rs	nars	nurse
-ks	viks	vicks
-rt	Bert	Bert
-ks	kyúteks	cutex

Clusters in medial position:

n-ts	mantsa	stain
n-dr	londri	laundry
n-tr	kontrata	contract
ng-gr	konggreso	congress
s-kw	eskwela	school
m-br	sombrero	hat
l-kr	sepulkro	sepulchre
m-pl	timpla	flavor
n-kl	konklusyon	conclusion

Final and initial clusters (across syllable boundaries):

ns-tr	konstruksyon	construction
ks-tr	ekstra	extra

5. Stress and Vowel Length

Tagalog has stressed (marked ´) or unstressed (unmarked) syllables.

Stress in Tagalog is usually on the last two syllables of the word. But it needs an exhaustive study to find out on which of these two syllables it falls in any particular word.

Stressed syllables, except for final ones, are accompanied by vowel length:

báhay	[bá:hay]	house
butás	[butás]	punctured
maglálaba	[maglá:laba]	will wash (clothes)
umaáwit	[umaá:wit]	is singing
pambútas	[pambú:tas]	instrument for making holes

The following pairs of words show that a shift in

stress results in a difference in meaning.

First Syllable (´)		Second Syllable (´)	
áso [á:so]	dog	asó [asó]	smoke
bálat [bá:lat]	birthmark	balát [balát]	skin
búkas [bú:kas]	tomorrow	bukás [bukás]	open
káyo [ká:yo]	a piece of cloth	kayó [kayó]	you (pl)
gábi [gá:bi]	yam	gabí [gabí]	night
gútom [gú:tom]	hunger	gutóm [gutóm]	hungry
hámon [há:mon]	a dare	hamón [hamón]	ham
páko' [pá:ko']	nail	pakó' [pakó']	fern
páso' [pá:so']	a burn	pasó' [pasó']	flower pot
sáya [sá:ya]	skirt	sayá [sayá]	gaiety
túbo [tú:bo]	pipe	tubó [tubó]	sugar cane

When a suffix is added to a word stressed on the second to the last syllable (penultimate stress), the stress is shifted to the next syllable following it:

> bása   →   basáhin
>
> paglínis →   paglinísin

When stressed on the last syllable (ultimate stress), the stress is usually shifted to the suffix.

> bilí   →   bilhín
>
> dalá   →   dalhín
>
> walís   →   walisín
>
> puntá →   puntahán

6. Pitch and Intonation Contours

There are three kinds of pitches in Tagalog. The three levels may be indicated as follows:

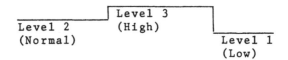

Level 3
(High)

Level 2
(Normal)

Level 1
(Low)

Tagalog sentences have very slight variations in pitch. The sentences usually start off with level 2, the normal pitch, going up slightly over stressed syllables, reaching level 3 when the sentence is a question or ending in level 2 or 1 at the end of statements.

There are three kinds of intonation contours for Tagalog sentences. They are Rising for questions and requests; Falling or Level for statements, commands, and responses; and Suspended for series and non-final phrases. Interrogative questions, tag questions, and requests often end with a rise rather than a fall. Non-final phrases too, often end in a slight rise. Examples follow:

Statements

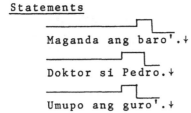

Maganda ang baro'.↓

Doktor si Pedro.↓

Umupo ang guro'.↓

Questions

Yes-no questions

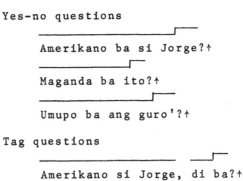

Amerikano ba si Jorge?↑

Maganda ba ito?↑

Umupo ba ang guro'?↑

Tag questions

Amerikano si Jorge, di ba?↑

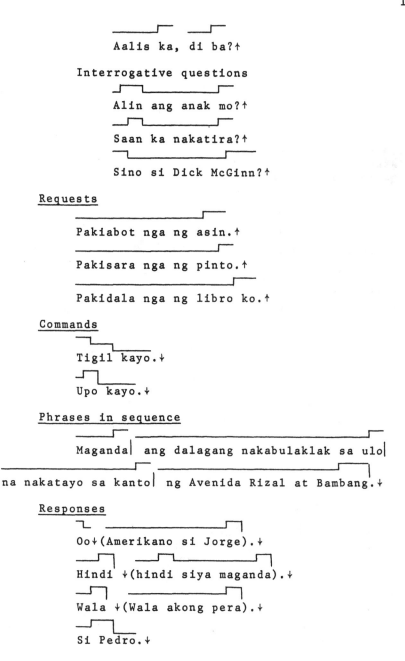

Aalis ka, di ba?↑

Interrogative questions

Alin ang anak mo?↑

Saan ka nakatira?↑

Sino si Dick McGinn?↑

Requests

Pakiabot nga ng asin.↑

Pakisara nga ng pinto.↑

Pakidala nga ng libro ko.↑

Commands

Tigil kayo.↓

Upo kayo.↓

Phrases in sequence

Maganda| ang dalagang nakabulaklak sa ulo|
na nakatayo sa kanto| ng Avenida Rizal at Bambang.↓

Responses

Oo↓(Amerikano si Jorge).↓

Hindi ↓(hindi siya maganda).↓

Wala ↓(Wala akong pera).↓

Si Pedro.↓

II. WORD FORMATION

1. Composition of Words

1.1 Roots vs. Stems

Words are either roots or stems. A root or base
is a simple word without any formative element or affix.
A stem on the other hand is composed of a root and one
or more affixes. Examples of roots and stems follow:

Root		Stems	
lákad	walk	l-um-ákad	to walk
súlat	write	pang-súlat	used for writing
asáwa	spouse	mag-asáwa	to get married
upó'	sit	upu-án	seat
laró'	play	pag-laró'	playing

Particles are types of roots that are usually
monosyllabic and do not generally take affixes.

Pronouns: ko, mo, akin, iyo, namin, ito, nito

Adverbial particles: pa, na, lang, naman

Markers: ang, ng, sa, ay

Interjections: ay, naku, sus, sayang

Conjunctions: kaya, dahil, at, nguni't, o, pero

1.2 Reduplication

Words can be reduplicated, that is one or more
syllables at the beginning of the full word may be
repeated. Examples of different types of reduplication
follow.

Partial reduplication

One syllable near the beginning of the word may be
reduplicated. This syllable is either the first syllable

of the root or part of a compound affix. What is reduplicated is either the first vowel of a word that
starts with a vowel or the first consonant and vowel
if the word starts with a consonant.

Root	Partial Reduplicated Form	
lakad	la-lakad	will walk
	mag-pa-pa-lakad	will make something run
iyak	i-iyak	will cry
	nag-i-i-iyak	crying re-peatedly
suntok	su-suntok-in	will box (something)
	s-um-u-suntok	is/are boxing

Full reduplication

The whole word or root may be reduplicated.

Root/Stem		Full Reduplicated Form	
araw	day, sun	araw-araw	every day
isa	one	isa-isa	one by one
ma-taba'	stout, fat	mataba-taba'	very stout, fat
ma-ganda	beautiful	maganda-ganda	very beautiful

Combined partial and full reduplication

A part and a whole word are repeated in one form.

Root		Reduplicated Form	
isa	one	i-isa-isa	only one
dalawa	two	da-dalawa-dalawa	only two
tawa	laugh	ta-tawa-tawa	laughing

tanga	stupid	ta-tanga-tanga	being stupid
awat	stop	a-awat-awat	stopping (a fight)

Sometimes when there are more than two syllables to a root, only the first two syllables are reduplicated.

Root		Reduplicated Form	
sigarilyo	cigarette	si-siga-sigarilyo	smoking a cigarette
baligtad	turned over	ba-bali-baligtad	turning over
usisa'	to inquire	u-usi-usisa'	inquiring

1.3 Compounding

Certain words can be formed by compounding, the resultant forms having a different meaning from the two roots.

batong-buhay	white stone
dahong-palay	name of a poisonous snake
bahay-bata	ovary
anak-araw	albino
hampas-lupa	tramp, bum
bigay-loob	gift
bigay-kaya	dowry
bantay-salakay	opportunist
basag-ulo	trouble
balat-sibuyas	sensitive, smooth complexion

2. Parts of Speech

Parts of speech are divided into nine classes according to their uses in sentences. They are the following: Nouns, Verbs, Pronouns (Personal, Demonstrative, Interrogative, and Indefinite), Adjectives (Ma adjectives and Unaffixed adjectives), Quantifiers, Numerals, Adverbs, Markers (Relational and Non-relational), and Interjections.

2.1 Nouns

Nouns may be roots:

báta'	child
báhay	house
áso	dog
bundók	mountain
bató	stone

They may be a combination of a root and a noun forming affix:

taga + lúto'	cook or one who cooks
upu + án	seat
ka + ligayá + han	happiness
pag + káin	food

There are two types of nouns: <u>count nouns</u>, or nouns that can be counted like <u>silya</u> 'chair', <u>lapis</u> 'pencil' etc., and <u>mass nouns</u> or nouns that cannot be counted. Examples of mass nouns are the following:

Sand-like Elements

asín	salt
pamintá	pepper
gawgáw	starch
harína	flour
asúkal	sugar
lúpa'	soil
buhángin	sand
alikabók	dust

Cereals

bigás	rice
monggó	mongo beans
maís	corn
darák	rice bran
pálay	unhusked rice
malagkít	glutinous rice

Liquids

gátas	milk
túbig	water
kapé	coffee
tsokoláte	chocolate
tsaá	tea
salabát	ginger tea

Metals

pílak	silver
gintó'	gold
tansó'	copper
tinggá'	lead
bákal	iron

Food

karné	meat
pansít	noodles
úlam	viands
matamís	dessert

Sauces

patís	fish or shrimp sauce
súka'	vinegar

tóyo'	soy sauce

Dry Goods

búlak	cotton
papél	paper
téla	cloth
sinúlid	thread

Elements of Nature

asó	smoke
hángin	wind
kulóg	thunder
ulán	rain

Mass nouns cannot be preceded by the pluralizer mga since they do not indicate plurality of number.

Mass nouns differ from count nouns in that a numeral cannot precede them without a quantifier in between. Note the following:

isang dakot na bigas	one handful of rice
daluwang salop na tsaa	two gantas of tea
isang sakong palay	one sack of unhusked rice

In each case the order is numeral + quantifier + linker + mass noun.

Mass nouns, too, can only be used after the interrogative pronoun gaano and never after the interrogative countable pronoun ilan: Gaanong bigas.... 'How much rice....', but not *Ilang bigas.... 'How many rice...'.

When mass nouns are preceded by quantifiers, they are included in a phrase that can occur with ilan: Ilang salop na bigas.... 'How many gantas of rice....'.

Nouns can also be classified as common nouns and proper nouns. Common nouns are preceded by the noun markers ang, ng, sa; proper nouns or names are preceded

by si, ni, and kay. The following are examples: ang
bata' 'the child', si Pedro 'Peter'.

Common nouns are pluralized by adding the particle
mga before the noun it modifies. Proper nouns are
pluralized by changing si to sina. Thus ang mga [manga]
bata' 'children' and sina Pedro 'Peter and those with
him'.

Names of places, mountains, rivers and other proper
non-personal nouns are treated like common nouns and
have the common noun markers: Ang Maynila (name of a
city), ng Mayon (name of a volcano), sa Mataas na
Paaralang Arellano (name of a high school).

Common nouns like nanay 'mother' sometimes may take
the proper noun marker si instead of ang when they are
used as a name.

Names of animals are given personal attributes and
are marked by personal noun markers: Si Bantay 'Guard',
Ni Puti' 'Whitey', Kay Tagpi' 'Spot'.

When nouns are not marked by ang, ng, and sa, they
are indefinite: Bata ang umiyak. 'A child cried.'

Nouns used as comments or predicates usually occur
without noun markers: Doktor ang lalake. 'The man is a
doctor.', Direktor si Al White. 'Al White is a director.'

Nouns are used without the noun markers in the
vocative: Oy Pedro! 'Hey, Pedro!', Oy lalake! 'Hey,
Man!'

There are some Tagalog nouns affixed with ka- + -an
that fall within the category of mass nouns because
they are not countable. This type of noun can occur
with the marker ang and denote the quality or some
concept found in the base. These nouns are called
abstract nouns:

Ang ka-tapang-an	The bravery
Ang ka-ligaya-han	The happiness
Ang ka-sipag-an	The industriousness

Gender is not usually marked in Tagalog nouns.
The sex of a noun is often determined by the context in
which it is used or by putting the words lalake 'man'
or babae 'woman' after the noun and connecting them by
the linker:

kapatid na babae   sister

anak na lalake   son

pinsang babae   girl cousin

pamangkin na lalake   nephew

Some nouns, mostly Spanish borrowings, however,
mark gender like the following:

Masculine		Feminine	
direktor	director	direktora	directress
manong	elder brother	manang	elder sister
senyor	master	senyora	mistress
tiyo	uncle	tiya	aunt
maestro	teacher	maestra	teacher
konsehal	councilor	konsehala	councilor
doktor	doctor	doktora	doctor
abogado	lawyer	abogada	lawyer
padrino	godfather	padrina	godmother
ninong	godfather	ninang	godmother
kompadre	male sponsor	komadre	female sponsor
konduktor	conductor	konduktora	conductress
propesor	professor	propesora	professor

Note that o usually marks masculine gender and a,
feminine gender.

2.2 Verbs

A Tagalog verb usually contains a root or base and
one or more affixes. The base provides the meaning of
the verb whereas the affixes show the relation of the

topic to the verb and also the character of the action.

Verbs are classified by the affixes they take.
The affixes indicate which complement of the sentence is
in focus. A complement may be the <u>actor</u>, the <u>goal</u>, the
<u>location</u>, the <u>instrument</u> or the <u>beneficiary</u> of the
action. An affix, however, may mark more than one kind
of complement as in focus depending on the verb base,
but generally the following classification holds true
(the complement in focus is in parentheses).

(1) <u>Mag-/Um-</u> verbs indicate that the <u>actor</u> of the
sentence is in focus: <u>Bumili</u> (<u>ka</u>) <u>ng</u> <u>tinapay</u> <u>sa</u>
<u>tindahan</u> <u>para</u> <u>sa</u> <u>akin</u>. '(You) buy bread at the store for
me.'

(2) -<u>In</u> verbs usually indicate that the <u>goal</u> of the
sentence is in focus: <u>Bilhin</u> <u>mo</u> (<u>ang</u> <u>tinapay</u>) <u>sa</u>
<u>tindahan</u> <u>para</u> <u>sa</u> <u>akin</u>. 'Buy (bread) at the store for
me.'

(3) -<u>An</u> verbs usually indicate that the <u>location</u>
is in focus: <u>Bilhan</u> <u>mo</u> <u>ng</u> <u>tinapay</u> (<u>ang</u> <u>tindahan</u>). 'Buy
bread (at the store).'

(4) <u>Ipang-</u> verbs indicate that the <u>instrument</u> of
the sentence is in focus: <u>Ipangbili</u> <u>mo</u> <u>ng</u> <u>tinapay</u> <u>sa</u>
<u>tindahan</u> (<u>ang</u> <u>pera</u> <u>ko</u>). 'Buy bread at the store (with
my money).'

(5) <u>I-/Ipag-</u> verbs usually indicate that the
<u>beneficiary</u> is in focus: <u>Ibili</u> <u>mo</u> (<u>ako</u>) <u>ng</u> <u>tinapay</u> <u>sa</u>
<u>tindahan</u>. 'Buy bread (for me) at the store.'

Verbs inflect for <u>aspect</u> rather than tense as in
English. Aspect indicates whether the action has
started or has been completed. The three aspects are
(1) <u>completed</u> (action started and terminated), (2) <u>con-</u>
<u>templated</u> (action not started but anticipated),
(3) <u>incompleted</u> (action started but not yet completed
or action still in progress). The form of the verb
that does not imply any aspect is <u>neutral</u> or is in the
<u>infinitive</u> form. It is also the command or the im-
perative form of the verb. The following paradigm
gives the changes in verbal formation corresponding to
aspects.

Base: <u>Sulat</u> 'write'

Aspect	Mag- Verb	Um- Verb
Neutral (Infinitive)	magsulát	sumúlat
Completed (Past)	nagsulát	sumúlat
Incompleted (Progressive)	nagsusulát	sumusúlat
Contemplated (Future)	magsusulát	susúlat

A more detailed description of these changes will be discussed in section 3.

Verbs can be classified into <u>causative</u> and <u>non-causative</u> (indicative) forms. Causative verbs add <u>pa</u> to mean 'to cause, make, or have someone do something'. There are two actors in a causative sentence: the <u>causer</u> of the action and the <u>agent</u> caused to perform the action. Examples of causative and indicative sentences are as follows:

<u>Indicative</u>	Naglaba ako ng damit.	I washed the clothes.
<u>Causative</u>	Nagpalaba ako ng damit sa labandera.	I had the wash woman launder the clothes.

2.3 Pronouns

Pronouns as substitutes for nouns may be classified into the following types.

2.31 Personal Pronouns

The personal pronouns may be divided into <u>ang</u>-pronouns (substitutes for noun phrases marked by <u>ang</u>), <u>ng</u> pronouns (substitutes for noun phrases introduced by <u>ng</u>), and <u>sa</u> pronouns (substitutes for noun phrases introduced by <u>sa</u>).

(1) The <u>Ang</u> pronouns.

The forms of the <u>ang</u> pronouns are the following:

Person	Singular		Plural	
First	akó	I	kamí	(exclusive) we (I and others)
			táyo	(inclusive) we (I, you, and others)
Second	ikáw, ka	you	kayó	you (plural)
Third	siyá	he/she	silá	they

Ikaw, 'you (singular)' is a variant form of ka. It usually occurs initially in sentences while ka occurs elsewhere: Ikaw ba si Pedro? 'Are you Pedro?' and Si Pedro ka ba? also 'Are you Pedro?'

Unlike in English, gender is not distinguished in the third person, singular form of the Tagalog personal pronoun.

Note the English translation 'we' for both the first person exclusive kamí and the first person inclusive táyo. Kamí refers to the speakers and others, excluding the person spoken to. Táyo refers to everybody--including the one spoken to.

(2) The Ng pronouns.

The forms of the ng pronouns are the following:

Person	Singular		Plural	
First	ko	I	namin	(exclusive) we
			natin	(inclusive) we
Second	mo	you	ninyo	you (plural)
Third	niya	he/she	nila	they

Notice that the ng pronouns have the same gloss as the ang pronouns. When these pronouns follow nouns immediately, they act as possessive adjectives.

bahay ko	my house
bahay niya	his house
bahay ninyo	your house

When a verb precedes these ng pronouns, the pronouns function as actors in the sentence: Ano ang ginawa mo? 'What did you do?'

(3) The Sa pronouns.

The forms of the sa pronouns are as follows:

Person	Singular		Plural	
First	akin	my; mine	amin	(exclusive) our; ours
			atin	(inclusive) our; ours
Second	iyo	your; yours	inyo	your; yours
Third	kaniya	his/her; his/hers	kanila	their; theirs

Sa pronouns may indicate possession or location. Unlike the other types of personal pronouns, the marker sa occurs obligatorily when the sa pronouns fill a locative complement slot and optionally when used to indicate possession.

Only the plural forms of the sa pronouns can be used to indicate location or place.

sa amin (exclusive)	from/to/at our place
sa atin (inclusive)	
sa inyo	from/to/at your place
sa kanila	from/to/at their place

2.32 Demonstrative Pronouns

The demonstrative pronouns indicate the relative distance of objects from the speaker and the listener. These pronouns may be divided into ang demonstratives, ng demonstratives and sa demonstratives.

(1) The Ang demonstratives.

The following demonstrative pronouns are

identified as the <u>ang</u> demonstratives.

<u>Ito</u> 'this' indicates that what is spoken of is nearer the speaker than the listener or near to both.

<u>Iyan</u> 'this' indicates that the object spoken about is near the listener and far from the speaker or a short distance away from both.

<u>Iyon</u> 'that, yonder' indicates that the object is far from both speaker and listener or farther away than that indicated by <u>iyan</u>.

<u>Iri</u> 'this one here' is sometimes used. It indicates that what is spoken of is very near the speaker.

This set of <u>ang</u> demonstratives fills the same position as the rest of the <u>ang</u> phrases and <u>ang</u> pronouns:

Ito		This	
Ang babae	ang nanay ko.	The woman	is my mother.
Siya		She	

(2) The <u>Ng</u> demonstratives.

The <u>ng</u> demonstratives are as follows:

nito	this (near the speaker and far from hearer or near to both)
niyan	that (far from speaker but close to hearer or far from both)
niyon/noon	that, over there; that, yonder (farther away from both)

The <u>ng</u> demonstratives fill the same position as the <u>ng</u> phrases and <u>ng</u> pronouns.

	nito?		the name of this?
Ano ang pangalan	ng doktor?	What's	the doctor's name?
	niya?		his name?

(3) The <u>Sa</u> demonstratives.

The demonstrative pronouns that can replace locative phrases marked by <u>sa</u> are <u>dito</u>, <u>diyan</u> and <u>doon</u>. They are referred to as <u>sa</u> demonstratives. The relative distances indicated by each of the demonstratives are the same as those of the <u>ang</u> demonstratives.

<u>Dito</u> 'here' indicates that the place or location is near the speaker or near to both the speaker and the listener.

<u>Diyan</u> 'there' signals that the place or location is far from the speaker but near the listener or it may also mean far from both.

<u>Doon</u> 'over there; there yonder' shows that the location of something is definitely farther away from both the speaker and the listener.

The variant forms <u>rito</u>, <u>riyan</u>, and <u>roon</u> are often used when what precedes them is a vowel sound.

Unlike <u>sa</u> pronouns, the <u>sa</u> demonstratives are not preceded by <u>sa</u>.

Pumunta siya
$\begin{bmatrix} \text{doon.} \\ \text{sa bahay ko.} \\ \text{sa amin.} \end{bmatrix}$
He went
$\begin{bmatrix} \text{there.} \\ \text{to my house.} \\ \text{to our place.} \end{bmatrix}$

2.33 Interrogative Pronouns

In general interrogatives consist of root particles. The most general examples are the following.

(1) <u>Sino</u> 'who' is a personal interrogative pronoun referring to persons. This interrogative word is answered by a <u>si</u> or an <u>ang</u> phrase of an identificational sentence (a sentence where both the topic (subject) and the comment (predicate) are marked by the definite article <u>ang</u> or <u>si</u>).

<u>Sino + Si phrase</u>

Question: <u>Sino</u> si Dick McGinn?
'Who is Dick McGinn?'

```
                    Topic               Comment
      Answer:   (Si Dick McGinn)    ang 'Country
                                        Director'.
                'Dick McGinn        is the Country
                                        Director.'
```

Sino + Ang phrase

```
      Question:   Sino ang 'Country Director'?
                  'Who is the Country Director?'
```

```
                    Topic               Comment
      Answer:   Si Dick McGinn      (ang 'Country
                                        Director').
                'Dick McGinn        is the Country
                                        Director.'
```

The plural form of sino is the reduplicated form sinu-sino. (Note the raising of o to u in non-final position when sino is reduplicated.)

A sinu-sino question is answered by the plural proper noun marker sina.

```
      Question:   Sinu-sino ang mga guro sa Tagalog?
                  'Who are the Tagalog teachers?'
```

```
      Answer:   Sina Binibining Ros, Binibining Gallega
                at Ginoong Dytioco.
                'They are Miss Ros, Miss Gallega and Mr.
                Dytioco.'
```

(2) Ano 'what' is a neuter interrogative pronoun referring to things, activities and qualities. Unlike sino, ano is answered by unmarked comments.

```
      Question:   Ano ang kulay ng bulaklak?
                  'What's the color of the flower?'
```

```
      Answer:   Asul (ang kulay ng bulaklak).
                'Blue (is the color of the flower).'
```

```
      Question:   Ano ang ginawa niya?
                  'What did he do?'
```

```
      Answer:   Tumakbo (siya).
                'He ran.'
```

```
Question:  Ano ito?
           'What's this?'
Answer:    Lapis (iyan).
           'It's a pencil.'
```

The plural form of <u>ano</u> is <u>anu-ano</u>. Like <u>sinu-sino</u>, <u>anu-ano</u> is answered by a series of objects, activities, qualities, etc.

<u>Ano</u> may be used as a tag question.

```
           Maganda siya, ano?
           'She's beautiful, isn't she?'
```

(3) <u>Alin</u> 'which' refers to either persons or things. This interrogative word is answered by definite statements beginning with <u>ito/iyan/iyon</u>.

```
Question:  Alin ang lapis mo?    Which is your pen-
                                   cil?
Answer:    Ito (ang lapis ko).    This (is my pen-
                                   cil).
```

<u>Alin-alin</u> is the plural form of <u>alin</u>.

(4) <u>Kanino</u> 'whose' is answered by <u>ng</u> phrases or their substitutes and <u>sa</u> pronouns to indicate possession.

```
Question:  Kaninong lapis ito?    Whose pencil is
                                    this?
          ┌ (Sa) akin.           ┌ Mine.
Answer:   │ Lapis ko.            │ My pencil.
          └ Lapis ng estudyante. └ The student's
                                    pencil.
```

The reduplication of the first two syllables of <u>kanino</u> results in its plural form <u>kani-kanino</u>.

<u>Para kanino</u> 'for whom' is answered by benefactive phrases marked by <u>para sa/kay</u>.

```
Q:  Para kanino ang sapatos?    For whom are these
                                shoes?

A:          ⎡Tatay.              ⎡Father.
    Para sa |bata.          For |the child.
            |akin.               |me.
    Para kay Cely.               ⎣Cely.
```

(5) Ilan 'how many' occurs before count nouns. It is often answered by numerals indicating quantity.

```
Q:  Ilan ang anak mo?       How many children do
                            you have?

A:  Tatlo (ang anak ko).    Three (are my children).
```

(6) Gaano 'how much' unlike ilan occurs before mass nouns (non-countable nouns). This interrogative word is usually answered by mass nouns preceded by quantifiers.

```
Q:  Gaanong bigas ang       How much rice do you
        kailangan mo?       need?

A:  Tatlong salop (na       Three gantas (of rice
        bigas ang kailangan     are what I need).
        ko).
```

(7) Magkano 'how much' is used in buying and selling. It is answered by the price of the object being bought.

```
Q:  Magkano ang manok?      How much is the
                            chicken?

A:  Dos singkuwenta.        Two-fifty.
```

When partially reduplicated to magkakano this word acquires a distributive meaning 'how much each or a piece'. The response to magkakano reflects the distributive meaning of 'so much a piece' because of the prefix tig-.

```
Q:  Magkakano ang pakwan?   How much is each
                            watermelon?

A:  Tig-alawang piso.       Two pesos each.
```

(8) <u>Kailan</u> 'when' questions are answered by time expressions.

Q: <u>Kailan</u> ang dating niya?   When is he coming?

A: Sa a-singko ng Mayo   On May fifth.

   Sa Mayo.   In May.

   Sa Sabado.   On Saturday.

   Bukas.   Tomorrow.

   Mamaya.   Later on.

(9) <u>Saan</u> 'where' is answered by locative phrases marked by <u>sa</u>.

Q: <u>Saan</u> ang bahay mo?   Where is your house?

A: <u>Sa kanto</u>.   At the corner.

(a) <u>Saan sa</u> 'where at/in' asks for a more specific location. The answer is usually a <u>sa</u> phrase.

Q: <u>Saan sa</u> Pilipinas   Where in the Philip-
    ang Mayon?   pines is Mayon
                     (Volcano)?

A: Sa Albay.   In Albay.

Q: <u>Saan sa</u> Albay?   Where in Albay?

A: Sa Legaspi.   In Legaspi.

(b) <u>Taga-saan</u> 'from where or from what place' is answered by <u>taga-</u> plus the place name where one is from.

Q: <u>Taga-saan</u> ka?

A: <u>Taga-</u> Maynila.

(c) <u>Nasaan</u> 'where' is answered by specific locative phrases marked by <u>na</u> plus <u>sa</u>-complements or phrases and their substitutes.

Q: <u>Nasaan</u> ang relo mo? Where's the watch?

```
A:  Nasa ibabaw ng mesa.    On the table.

    Nasa akin.              With me.

    Na kay Cres.            With Cres.

    Na kina Cres.           With Cres (and her
                            companions).

    Na rito.     Nan dito.  Here.

    Na riyan.  or Nan diyan. There.

    Na roon.     Nan doon.  Over there.
```

(10) Paano 'how' is usually answered by adverbs of manner.

```
Q:  Paano siya lumakad?     How did he walk?

A:  Lumakad siya nang       He walked on his
    paluhod.                knees.

    Paganito.               This way.
```

(11) Bakit 'why' elicits a response introduced by dahil, sapagka't or kasi 'because'--a statement of purpose or reason.

```
Q:  Bakit siya pumunta sa   Why did he go to the
    airport?                airport?

A:  Kasi  ]
    Dahil  } darating ang   Because his cousin is
              pinsan ko.    coming.
    Sapagka't]
```

Except for kailan and bakit, all of the interrogative pronouns listed above are followed by the linker -ng when immediately preceding a noun.

2.34 Indefinite Pronouns

(1) Some indefinite pronouns may be unaffixed forms. The following illustrate.

Kuwan 'such and such; so and so' (a cover term for anything in the language--a 'whatchamacallit'): Kinuha na niya yong kuwan. 'He already got the kuwan.'

Iba 'other': Nasaan ang iba? 'Where are the others?'

Kapwa 'both, fellow': Kapwa may kotse. 'Both of them have cars.'

Isa 'one, other (of two)': Isa ang natira. 'One was left.'

Lahat 'all': Dumating ang lahat. 'All of them came.'

Marami 'many': Marami ang kinumbida. 'Many were invited.'

Kaunti 'little, few': Kaunti lang ang kinain niya. 'He ate only a little.'

Other indefinite pronouns are kulang 'less', ilan 'some', sarili 'self'. In most cases these pronouns are used as pronominal adjectives; that is, they modify the nouns that immediately follow them.

(2) Some indefinite pronouns have the affix -man '-body, -thing' suffixed to certain interrogative pronouns.

Sinuman 'anybody, somebody, whoever': Sinuman ang kumuha ay nakatakbo na. 'Whoever took it had already escaped.'

Anuman 'something, anything, whatever': Anuman ang gawin mo ay huli na. 'Whatever you do now, it's too late.'

Alinman 'anybody, anything, whichever': Kunin mo alinman ang gusto mo. 'Take whichever you want.'

2.4 Adjectives

Adjective Formation

Root words which are quality or descriptive words are classified as adjectives. Examples of these adjectival base words follow.

pangit	ugly
payat	thin
tamad	lazy
lúma	not new, old
bago	new

Other adjectives are formed by adding the prefix
ma- to a root. In these cases the words assume the
meaning 'having or being full of' what is expressed by
the root.

gandá	beauty	ma- + ganda	beautiful
ínit	heat	ma- + ínit	hot
yáman	wealth	ma- + yáman	wealthy

The ma- adjectives can be classified into three
kinds.

(1) Noun Modifiers Only.

Some adjectives modify nouns only.

mataas na máma'	the man is tall
mataba-ng babae	the woman is fat

Note the use of the linker na/-ng before the noun.
Na is used when preceded by a consonant (except n), and
-ng is attached to the adjective when preceded by vowels
and n (with n replaced by ng). The pre-noun position
of adjectives is not fixed (except for a very few cases).
It can usually alternate freely before or after the
noun modified.

(2) Verbal Modifiers Only.

Some ma- adjectives function like adverbs of
manner in English because they modify verbs. In Tagalog
however these adjectives have very limited occurrence.
They appear only before infinitive forms of the verbs.

ma-bilís tumakbo	to run fast
ma-bágal maglaba	to wash (clothes) slowly

ma-húsay manahi   to sew well

ma-dalás magsimba   to go to church frequently

Other examples are <u>mainam</u>, <u>maluwat</u>, etc.

(3) Both Nouns and Verbal Modifiers.

Other <u>ma-</u> adjectives, however, can modify both
nouns and verbs.

maganda-ng	[babae	beautiful woman
	[ngumiti'	to smile beautifully
magaling na	[maestra	good teacher
(na)	[magsalita'	to speak well
marunong na	[estudyante	intelligent student
(na)	[sumagot	to answer intelligently
mahirap na	[tao	poor person
(na)	[magtrabaho	hard work
malakas na	[lalake	strong man
(na)	[kumain	to eat a lot

Note that <u>na</u> is optional or is often deleted before
verbs but not before nouns. -<u>Ng</u> however is always
present.

Pluralization

<u>Ma-</u> adjectives may express plurality when a plural
meaning of the noun being modified is suggested. The
plural form is indicated by a reduplication of the first
syllable (CV-/V-) of the adjective base.

Adjective Base	Ma- Adjective (singular)		Ma- Adjective (plural)
liít	maliít	small	maliliít
ásim	maásim	sour	maaásim

The plural particle <u>mga</u> before the adjective is
enough however to express plurality.

Singular: malaking mangga   big mango

Plural: malalaking mangga   big mangoes
           mga malalaking mangga
           <u>mga malaking mangga</u>

To express the same degree of quality in nouns
being compared, the adjectival root is preceded by
<u>magkasing</u> or <u>kasing</u>.

Positive Degree		Degree of Equality			
maputí'	white	<u>magkasing</u>	putí'	equally	white
matabá'	fat	<u>kasing</u>	tabá'		fat
mataás	tall		taás		tall
mabaít	good		baít		good
pángit	ugly		pángit		ugly
bágo	new		bágo		new

Note the loss of the prefix <u>ma</u>- after the
equalizers.

The comparative degree of adjectives is expressed
by the use of the comparative particles <u>mas</u>, <u>lalong</u>,
and <u>higit</u> <u>na</u> 'more, -er'.

Positive Degree	Comparative Degree		
maganda 'beautiful'	<u>mas</u>	maganda	more beautiful
mainit 'hot'	<u>lalo-ng</u>	mainit	hotter
mura 'cheap'	<u>higit na</u>	mura	cheaper
popular 'popular'		popular	more popular

The superlative degree of the adjective is expressed by the affix <u>pinaka</u>- 'most, -est' prefixed to
the positive forms of the adjectives.

Positive Degree	Superlative Degree	
ma+ganda	pinaka-maganda	most beautiful
ma+init	pinaka-mainit	hottest
popular	pinaka-popular	most popular
mura	pinaka-mura	cheapest

The absolute superlative, or high degree of the quality without specific comparison is expressed in the following ways.

(1) The adjectives are modified by the adverbs lubha', di hamak 'much more'.

```
di hamak na ⎤                (na di hamak)      much more
            ⎥ magaling                             excellent
lubha-ng    ⎦                (na lubha)
```

The adverbs may occur before or after the adjective modified.

(2) To express high intensity of the quality, the adjective roots are preceded by the following:

```
sukdulan ng ⎤
            ⎥
ubod ng     ⎥ ganda              very beautiful
            ⎥
napaka-     ⎦
```

(3) The high intensity of the quality is also expressed when the adjectives are repeated, the two being joined by the linker.

magaling na magaling	very good
maganda-ng maganda	very beautiful
pangit na pangit	very ugly
bago-ng bago	very new

2.5 Quantifiers

There are some common nouns that may act as modifiers to noun heads. These are nouns of quantity or quantifiers. Tagalog has a long list of these quantifiers which are understood in terms of collections, measures, or sub-parts of objects. Some of these are not standard units of measure but approximations or rough calculations of quantity. For instance tumpok is a 'pile, heap, a group' usually used in selling tomatoes, garlic, onions, boiled sweet potatoes, etc.; gatang is a big tin can of milk used as a measure of cereals in small quantities.

When these quantifiers occur before mass nouns, they are preceded by numerals thus converting mass nouns into count nouns. The order is quite fixed: the numeral occurs first, followed by the quantifier and then by the noun modified.

Numeral	Quantifiers	Noun
dalawang 'two'	yarda 'yards'	
dalawang 'two'	yardang 'yards of'	tela 'cloth'
apat na 'four'	latang 'cans of'	gatas 'milk'
isang 'one'	tumpok na 'pile of'	kamatis 'tomatoes'

Note the use of linkers after each modifier. Note, too, that the head noun may be deleted and when this happens the quantifier loses its linker and becomes the head of the construction.

Some of the common quantifiers follow.

isang salop na bigas	one ganta of rice
isang pirasong keso	one piece of cheese
isang kilong lansones	one kilo of lanzones
isang metrong tela	one meter of cloth
isang sakong palay	one sack of rice
isang kaing na mangga	one basket of mangoes
isang takal na monggo	one can of mongo (beans)

2.6 Numerals

The numerals like adjectives modify nouns, so they are subclassified as adjectives. Unlike adjectives though, the numerals always come before the nouns they modify. Like adjectives, numerals are linked to the words they modify by na/-ng.

isa-ng linggo	one week
dalawa-ng taon	two years
apat na buwan	four months

Numerals are grouped here into cardinals, ordinals, fractions, and distributives.

Cardinals

The cardinals from 'one' to 'ten' are as follows.

isá	one	ánim	six
dalawá	two	pitó	seven
tatló	three	waló	eight
ápat	four	siyám	nine
limá	five	sampú'	ten

In counting by tens, pu' is added to the cardinals.

sampu'	(isa+ng+pu')	ten or one ten
dalawampu'	(dalawa+ng+pu')	twenty or two tens
tatlumpu'	(tatlo+ng+pu')	thirty or three tens
apat na pu'		forty or four tens
limampu'	(lima+ng+pu')	fifty or five tens
anim na pu'		sixty or six tens
pitumpu'	(pito+ng+pu')	seventy or seven tens
walumpu'	(walo+ng+pu')	eighty or eight tens
siyam na pu'		ninety or nine tens

Note the use of the linker na/-ng to connect cardinal numeral construction. Na occurs after

consonants and -ng after vowels. -M, an alternate form
of -ng occurs before p sounds (see numbers 10, 20, 30,
70, 80 above).

Labi derived from labis 'more or over' is added to
the cardinals from isa 'one' to siyam 'nine' to mean
'eleven' to 'nineteen'.

labi-ng isa	(11)	labi-ng anim	(16)
labi-n dalawa	(12)	labi-m pito	(17)
labi-n tatlo	(13)	labi-ng walo	(18)
labi-ng apat	(14)	labi-n siyam	(19)
labi-n lima	(15)		

Note that the linker -ng attached to labi- connects
the cardinal numeral constructions. However, depending
upon the following sound, the -ng may have the -n or -m
alternate forms.

-ng before vowel sounds and w (see numbers 11,
     13, 16, and 18 above).

-n   before d, t, l, or s sounds (see numbers 12,
     13, 15 and 19 above).

-m   before p (see number 17 above).

Daán means 'a unit of hundred'. Its variant form
when preceded by a vowel is raán.

isa-n daán	(100)	anim na raán	(600)
dalawa-n daán	(200)	pito-n daán	(700)
tatlo-n daán	(300)	walu-n daán	(800)
apat na raán	(400)	siyam na raán	(900)
lima-n daán	(500)		

Líbo means 'a unit of thousand'.

Milyón means 'a unit of million'

The conjunction at 'and' is used between two
numeral units put together to form another numeral that
is greater in value. When preceded by a vowel, at is

often contracted to 't.

$$\text{dalawampu} \begin{bmatrix} \text{'t} \\ \text{at} \end{bmatrix} \text{isá} \qquad (21)$$

siyam na raan at siyam na pu't lima   (995)

The Ordinals

The ordinals are formed by prefixing <u>ika-</u> to the cardinals except to <u>isa</u> 'one' where the Spanish <u>una</u> is used instead.

úna	first	ika-ánim	sixth
ika-lawá	second	ika-sampú'	tenth
ika-tló	third	ika-dalawampú't tatlo	twenty-third
iká-pat	fourth		
ika-limá	fifth	ika-(i) sandaán	hundredth
		ika-(i) sanlíbo	thousandth

Note the irregularity of <u>ikatlo</u> (<u>ika+tatlo</u>), <u>ikalawa</u> (<u>ika+dalawa</u>) and <u>ikapat</u> (<u>ika+apat</u>). The first syllable of each of these numerals is dropped.

<u>Pang-</u> may be used to replace <u>ika-</u>.

pangalawá	(pang+dalawa)	pampitó	(pang+pito)
pangatló	(pang+tatlo)	pangwaló	
pangápat	(pang+apat)	pansiyám	(pang+siyam)
panlimá	(pang+lima)	pansampú'	(pang+sampu')

Note that the first consonant of the cardinal is dropped in the forms for 'second' and 'third'.

For expressing dates, <u>a-</u> prefixed to Spanish numerals is used more often than <u>ika-</u> prefixed to Tagalog numerals. <u>A-</u> is a borrowing from Spanish, hence no Tagalog numeral occurs after this prefix.

a-síngko	the 5th	a-katórse	the 14th
a-béynte	the 20th	a-priméro	the first

Fractions

<u>Bahági'</u> is added after the <u>ika-</u> numerals to mean
'a part'.

isa-ng bahagi	one part
ika-lawa-ng bahagi	half, second part
ika-tlo-ng bahagi	third, third part
ika-lima-ng bahagi	fifth, fifth part
ika-anim na bahagi	sixth, sixth part

<u>Kaláhati'</u> is often used for 'one half' or 'half'.

Distributives

Reduplication of the cardinals signifies 'so many
at a time'.

isa-isá	one by one, one after another
dala-dalawá	two by two
lima-limá	five at a time
sampu-sampú'	ten at a time
labi-labing isá	eleven at a time
sanda-sandaán	a hundred at a time

Note that a maximum of two syllables at a time
may be reduplicated.

Reduplication of the first syllable of a numeral
signifies 'only so many'.

í-isá	only one	pí-pitó	only seven
dá-dalawá	only two	wá-waló	only eight
tá-tatló	only three	sí-siyám	only nine
á-ápat	only four	sá-sampú'	only ten
lí-limá	only five	lá-labing isá	only eleven
á-ánim	only six	dá-dalawampú'	only twenty
		í-isandaán	only a hundred

Note that the reduplicated vowel sound is stressed.

Intensification of the restrictiveness of the numeral may be attained by both partial and full reduplication applied to the base.

í-isá-isá
'only one'

dá-dalawá-dalawá
'only two'

tá-tatló-tatló
'only three'

á-ápat-apát
'only four'

lí-limá-limá
'only five'

á-aním-aním
'only six'

pí-pitó-pitó
'only seven'

wá-walú-waló
'only eight'

sí-siyam-siyam
'only nine'

sá-sampú-sampú'
'only ten'

When the numeral is a non-base, the first part of the stem is reduplicated.

la-labin-labing-isa   only eleven

da-dalawa-dalawampu't isa   only twenty-one

i-isa-isandaan   only one hundred

By prefixing tig- to the cardinals, the combination signifies 'so many each or so many a piece'.

tig-ísa   one apiece, one each

tig-aláwa   two apiece, two each

tig-atló   three apiece, three each

tig-apat   four apiece, four each

The second and third forms drop the first consonant of the base.

To reinforce the meaning of distribution, the first to the fourth forms reduplicate the first two syllables.

tigi-tigí-sa
'one each'

tiga-tiga-láwa
'two each'

tiga-tiga-tló
'three each'

tiga-tigá-pat
'four each'

Apat 'four' plus the rest of the numerals reduplicate the first syllable of the base.

tig-a-ápat	four each	tig-wa-walú	eight each
tig-li-limá	five each	tig-si-siyám	nine each
tig-pi-pitó	seven each	tig-sa-sampú'	ten each

Prices, usually Spanish terms, get partially reduplicated, too, when referring to the prices of each of the items.

Price		Prices of Each
Síngko	(₱.05)	Tig-sisíngko 'five centavos each'
Diyés	(₱.10)	Tig-didiyés 'ten centavos each'
Dos-singkuwénta	(₱2.50)	Tig-dodos-singkuwenta 'Two-fifty each'
Kuwarénta	(₱.40)	Tig-kukuwarenta 'forty centavos each'

'One peso each' however has the affix ma- prefixed to piso. The m- of the affix influences the p- of piso to change to m, thus mamiso is the resulting form.

2.7 Adverbs

2.71 Adverbs of Manner

Ma- Adverbs.

Adverbs of manner are usually identical to the ma-verbal modifiers in form, except that they are always preceded by the adverbial marker nang and their occurrence is often after the verb which may be in any of its inflected forms.

Note the contrast below between the verbal modifiers and the adverbs of manner.

Verbal Modifier   Adverbs of Manner

Verbal Verb	+	Uninflected Verb	Inflected Verb	Adverbial Marker	Adverb of Manner
mabilis (na) bumasa... 'reads fast...'			...bumasa 'read fast'	nang	mabilis
mabagal (na) bumasa... 'reads slowly...'			...bumabasa 'reading slowly'	nang	mabagal
mahinang bumasa... 'reads slowly...'			...babasa 'will read slowly'	nang	mahina'

Ma- adjectives describe the stative habitual action expressed by the infinitive form of the verb, whereas the ma- adverb describes the verbal action.

Pa- Adverbs.

Other adverbs of manner (usually of position) can be formed by prefixing pa- to verb roots.

After the Verb

Lumakad siya nang paluhod.	He walked on his knees.
Natulog siya nang pabaluktot.	He slept in a curled up position.
Natutulog siya nang padapa.	He is sleeping on his stomach.
Matutulog siya nang paupo.	He will sleep sitting down.
Matutulog siya nang patihaya.	He will sleep flat on his back.

Before the Verb

Paluhod siyang lumakad.   (See meanings above.)

Pabaluktot		natulog.
Padapa	siyang	natutulog.
Paupo		matutulog.
Patihaya		matutulog.

46

Unlike ma- modifiers, pa- modifiers occur before
verbs that can be inflected for aspect.

When pa- is prefixed to ano 'what' it means 'how',
referring to the manner of action.

Paano siya nakawala?   How did he get away?

Ga- Adverbs.

Ga- prefixed to ng- demonstratives make up the ga-
adverbs. The ga- adverbs are ganito 'like this',
ganiyan 'like that', and ganoon 'like that yonder'.

Ganito				this way.
Ganyan	siyang sumayaw.	He dances		that way.
Ganoon				that way yonder.

When ga- is prefixed to ano, it means 'like what'
or 'how much', referring to quantity, dimension or
measurement.

Maka- Adverbial Numerals.

Maka- with numerals, with the exception of the
first, results in forms meaning 'so many times'.

The second and third are usually irregular.

maká-lawa	twice
maká-itló	thrice, three times
maká-ápat	four times
maká-lima	five times

Adverbial Particles Describing Manner of Action.

Some particles like bigla and agad may follow
or precede verbs.

Sumigaw na bigla...	Shouted suddenly
(or Biglang sumigaw)	
Tumulong agad...	Helped immediately
(or Agad na tumulong)	

2.72 Adverbs of Time

Definite Adverbs of Time.

Certain adverbs refer to a specific point in time.

The present is denoted by ngayon 'today, now'.

The past is indicated by the prefix ka- attached
to nouns of time or numeral adverbs (maka + number).

ka-hapon	yesterday
ka-gabi	last night
ka-nina	earlier, a while ago (very recent past)
ka-maka-lawa	day after tomorrow
ka-maka-lima	five days ago

Noon before days, months, or year means 'previous
time or time past'.

noon-g isang linggo	last week
noon-g Mayo	last May

Note the use of the linker after noon.

Noon can also precede ka- adverbs of time like
noong kamakalawa '(last) two days ago'.

Days in the future are expressed by bukas
'tomorrow'.

bukas ng [umaga, hapon, gabi]   tomorrow [morning, afternoon, night]

Sa before days, months, hours, or year means some
time to come.

sa [Lunes, Mayo, a las tres]   on Monday, in May, at three o'clock

Mamaya indicates 'later today', (a very recent future).

	hapon	this afternoon
mamaya ng	gabi	tonight

Distributive Adverbs of Time.

The idea of <u>every</u> as in 'every day', 'every week' etc., is indicated by the full repetition of the noun of time.

oras-oras	every hour
araw-araw	every day
lingu-linggo	every week
buwan-buwan	every month
taun-taon	every year

Note the sound change of <u>o</u> to <u>u</u> in the reduplicated form of <u>linggo</u> and <u>taon</u>.

<u>Tuwí'</u> is placed before the definite names of the days of the week or the months to mean 'every' too.

	Linggo	every Sunday
tuwi-ng	Mayo	every month of May

Note the use of the linker after <u>tuwí'</u>.

Indefinite Adverbs of Time.

Particles Describing Duration of Action.

<u>Na</u> is a particle often used after verbs with completed aspects to mean completion of the action.

<u>Pa</u> on the other hand is used after verbs with non-completed aspects to mean action still going on or action not started yet.

| Kumain na siya. | He has already eaten. |
| Kumakain pa siya. | He is still eating. |

Kakain pa siya.　　He will eat yet.　(He has
　　　　　　　　　　not started eating yet.)

Other Indefinite Adverbs of Time.

paráti (-ng) ⎤	
(pa)lági' (-ng) ⎦	always
tuwi (-ng)	every
bihira (-ng)	seldom
bago	before ⎤ (used before in-
pagkatapos	after ⎥ finitive verb
	⎦ forms only)
ulí'	again
nang	when
mamaya (-ng)	a short time afterwards, soon
sandali (-ng)	for a while
minsan (-ng)	once, at one time
samantala (-ng) ⎤	
habang ⎦	while

2.73 Adverbial Particles

The following are other adverbial particles which are frequently used.

Rejoinder naman 'too, also'; a contrast marker, 'while, but'. Naman never occurs in initial sentences. It marks the sentence as a response to a previous sentence or a transition to another subject, hence also a mild contrast.

Magandang umaga naman.　　Good morning (to you) too.

Kumanta si Maria at
　tumugtog naman si
　Pedro.

Maria sang while Pedro
　played (a musical
　instrument).

Mayaman nga siya pero
　kuripot naman.

(True) she's rich but
　she's stingy.

Respect particle po 'sir/ma'am': Magandang umaga po naman. 'Good morning (to you) too, sir.' Only the plural pronouns kayo and sila or their ng and sa substitutes can apply to the person addressed with po. Po is inserted right after the first full word of each sentence.

Amerikano po si Roger.	Roger is an American, (Sir).
Pilipino po ba kayo?	Are you a Filipino, (Sir)?
Hindi po siya Pilipino.	He's not a Filipino, (Sir).
Magandang umaga po naman.	Good morning (to you) too, (Sir).

(Magandang umaga is considered a unit, so po is inserted after umaga.)

Indirect statement marker daw 'according to, it is said'. Daw indicates that the sentence represents the saying of someone other than the speaker. Raw is a variant form of daw when it occurs after a vowel: Maganda raw si Maria. 'It is said that Maria is beautiful.'

Degree marker lang, lamang 'just, only': Guwapo nga ang lalake pero pandak lang. 'The man is handsome but he's short.' Sekretarya lang siya. 'She's only a secretary.' Lang modifying a noun or an adjective has a belittling connotation, a depreciation of one's self or one's accomplishments. Lang following ka- verbs signals recently completed action: Kararating lang niya. 'He just arrived.'

Confirmation marker nga 'really, certainly, truly': Oo, mabait nga siya. 'Yes (you're right), he's good.' Nga expresses confirmation, assertion or emphasis. Like naman, it is found in responses rather than initial sentences.

Rejoinder din 'also, too': Maganda rin siya. 'She's also beautiful.' Rin is a variant form of din when it occurs after a vowel. Man functions like din in: Ikaw man. 'You, too.'

Emphatic marker <u>pala</u>: Siyanga, pala... 'Look here...' <u>Pala</u> also expresses surprise at an unexpected event or happening: Oo, nga pala, ano? 'Yeah, that's right.' Aba, tapos ka na palang magtrabaho. 'Oh, so you have already finished working.'

Affirmative response <u>oo</u> 'yes': Oo, pupunta siya doon. 'Yes, he's going there.'

Negative marker <u>hindi'</u> 'no, not': Hindi siya pupunta bukas. 'He won't go tomorrow.'

Non-existence marker <u>wala'</u> 'not there': Wala siya doon. 'He isn't there.'

Existence marker <u>may</u>, <u>mayroon</u> 'there is/are': May/ Mayroóng tao sa loob. 'There's somebody inside.'

2.8 Markers

Markers are uninflected words with little or no meaning. They are used to indicate relationships among the elements or parts of a sentence. There are two types of markers: the relation markers and the non-relation markers.

2.81 Relation Markers

Relation markers are placed before nouns or noun phrases that function as complements to the verbs. There are two types of relation markers: the Non-topic Relation Markers or Non-focus Markers, and the Topic Relation Marker.

The Non-topic Relation Markers

In a simple verbal sentence in Tagalog, the verb is followed by a string of noun phrases or complements each with a relation marker. This relation marker indicates the case relationship of the noun phrase to the sentence. There are three non-topic relation markers: <u>ng</u>, <u>sa</u> and <u>para sa</u>.

<u>Ng</u> (pronounced <u>nang</u>) marks the noun phrase as either an actor, goal, or instrument complement to the verb.

52

Actor: Kinuha <u>ng bata</u> ang   <u>The child</u> got
            libro.   the book.

Goal: Kumuha ang bata   The child got
            <u>ng libro</u>.   <u>a book</u>.

Instru-   Pinukpok niya   She beat the laundry
  mental: <u>ng palupalo</u> ang   <u>with a wooden</u>
          damit.   <u>paddle</u>.

<u>Sa</u> marks the noun phrase as a locative complement.

      Kumuha ang bata ng libro   The child got a
         <u>sa mesa</u>.   book <u>from the</u>
                               <u>table</u>.

<u>Para sa</u> marks the noun phrase as a benefactive
complement.

      Bumili ako ng sapatos   I bought a pair of
       <u>para sa kaniya</u>.   shoes <u>for him</u>.

The Topic or Focus Relation Marker

Generally one noun phrase is marked as topic or
focus[1] of attention in a sentence. This is done by a
topic marker which has no case marking function. The
case relationship to the sentence of this topicalized
noun phrase is indicated instead by the verbal affix.
<u>Ang</u> is the focus or topic marker. (See the <u>ang</u> phrases
in the sentences above.)

Topic and non-topic markers are also indicated by
proper noun markers, pronouns, and demonstratives. The
following chart gives the corresponding forms of each.

---

[1]<u>Focus</u> and <u>Topic</u> are used synonymously.

		NON-FOCUS MARKER		FOCUS MARKER
COMMON NOUN MARKER	ng	sa	para sa	ang
PROPER (sg) NOUN MARKER (pl)	ni	kay	para kay	si
	nina	kina	para kina	sina
PRONOUNS (sg) 1	ko	(sa) akin	para sa akin	ako
2	mo	(sa) iyo	para sa iyo	ikaw, ka
3	niya	(sa) kaniya	para sa kaniya	siya
(pl) 1	namin	(sa) amin	para sa amin	kami
	natin	(sa) atin	para sa atin	tayo
2	ninyo	(sa) inyo	para sa inyo	kayo
3	nila	(sa) kanila	para sa kanila	sila
DEMONSTRA-TIVES	nito	dito	para dito	ito
	niyan	diyan	para diyan	iyan
	niyon	doon	para doon	iyon

2.82 Non-relation Markers

There are two kinds of non-relation markers: the comment marker ay and the conjunctions.

The Comment Marker ay.

The normal order of a Tagalog sentence is the comment (or predicate) followed by the topic (or subject), or the verb followed by the topic then the rest of the comment. When the normal order is inverted, that is, when the topic comes before the comment, the comment is marked off from the topic by ay. The

particle <u>ay</u> is sometimes referred to as the inversion
marker.

Normal order: Pupunta siya sa   They are going
bahay.   home.

Inverted order: Siya ay pupunta
sa bahay.

The Conjunctions.

The conjunctions join words, phrases or sentences
either of equal or unequal rank. There are two types
of conjunctions: the coordinators and the subordinators.

The coordinators join words, phrases, and sentences
of equal rank. Some of them are as follows.

<u>at</u> 'and'

Maganda, mabait at masunurin   Maria is beauti-
si Maria.   ful, good and
obedient.

Bumili siya ng malaking   He bought a big
bahay at bagong kotse.   house and a
new car.

Kumanta si Maria at   Maria sang and
tumugtog naman si Pedro.   Pedro played
(a musical
instrument).

<u>o</u> 'or'

Tutugtog siguro si Maria   Perhaps Maria will
ng piyano o kakanta.   play the piano or
sing.

<u>pero</u> 'but'

Maganda ang bahay pero   The house is
maliit lang.   beautiful but
small.

<u>upang</u> 'so that'

Matulog ka ng umaga upang   Go to bed early so
huwag kang mahuli.   you won't be late.

The subordinator joins sentences of unequal rank, one being dependent or subordinated to the other.

<u>nang</u> 'when'

Patay na ang kabayo nang dumating ang damo.	The horse was dead when the grass arrived.

<u>kung</u> 'if'

Kakanta ako kung kakanta ka.	I will sing if you do.

<u>bago</u> 'before'

Sunog na ang bahay bago dumating ang bombero.	The house burned down before the firemen came.

2.9 Interjections

Interjections are exclamatory words used to express sudden or strong feeling. Some interjections are the following.

Hoy	Hey (you)
Aba ⎤ Ay ⎦	Oh; Alas (sudden reproach or emphatic denial)
Naku (po)	Oh, Mother
Sayang	What a pity
Dali'	Quick
Aray⎤ Aruy⎦	Ouch
Siya na⎤ Tama na⎦	Enough
Tabí	Get back
Layas ⎤ Sulong⎦	Go away

Nakakayamot	
Nakakainis	How irritating
Nakakabuwisit	

Nakakasuya   How disgusting

3. Affixation in Word Bases

Affixes are bound forms attached to a root or word base. There are three kinds of affixes:

Prefix, attached before a root or stem;

mag- + abót → magabót   to hand over

Infix, inserted in the root or stem;

takbó + -um- → tumakbó   to run

Suffix, attached after a root or stem.

alís + -in → alisín   to remove

The hyphens indicate that the affix is prefixed (mag-), infixed (-um-) or suffixed (-in).

In certain cases, a combination of a prefix and a suffix occurs with a root. We will call this compound affixation: ma-+ kaín +-an 'place for eating'.

A root word does not have any affixed form whereas a stem may.

There are three main classes of affixes used in Tagalog: affixes used in the formation of verbs; affixes used in the formation of adjectives or descriptives; and affixes used in the formation of substantives or nouns.

3.1 Major Affixes Used in Verbal Formation

The Tagalog verb is formed by combining a root and an affix. The root contains the main lexical content of the verb, and the affix shows the relationship of the verb to the topic or to the focused complement as well as the kind of action involved.

Five kinds of action will be discussed in this chapter. They are (1) the indicative, (2) the distributive, (3) the aptative, (4) the social, and (5) the causative.

The indicative involves a single action directed toward a single object. The action is neutral.

The distributive indicates a habitual or professional action directed toward or 'distributed' over several people, things, or several ways.

The aptative indicates the ability or possibility of doing something.

The social indicates a polite or indirect way of requesting or describing an action.

The causative signifies that someone permits or causes an action to take place.

Verbs as a form class are differentiated from other form classes by being inflected for aspect, kind of action, and focus.

3.11 Actor Focus Affixes

Actor focus affixes point to the actor as the topic of the sentence.

There are three major actor focus verbal affixes in the indicative mode.

(1) The mag- affix indicates deliberation and comprehensiveness of the action. It usually has an added feature of transitiveness. Most of the sentences where mag- is used or where it contrasts with -um- have an obligatory object (commonly known as a direct object in English). Mag-, too, in contrast with -um- denotes action which is more external in nature.

Example

mag- + tayo' → magtayo'   to erect, build
      'stand'

Magtayo ka ng bahay.   Build a house.

(2) The -um- affix, in comparison to the mag- affix, is more casual, involuntary, and suggests internal action. It is mostly intransitive because an object is not necessary to complete the sentence.

Example

-um- + tayo' → tumayo   to stand
         'stand'

Tumayo ka.   Stand up.

Both -um- and mag- verbal affixes are dynamic or active in nature.

(3) The ma- affix has a less active, dynamic function. It is used more to state a condition, and is descriptive in nature. Ma- is also used as the major adjectival affix. A special set of verbs take the ma- affix. The verb stems are mostly adjectival in nature. They are also intransitive.

Example

ma- + pagod → mapagod   to get tired
         'tired'

Napagod ako.   I got tired.

When stressed, má- also indicates that the action is accidental, unconscious, involuntary and unintentional.

Example

ma- + dapa' → mádapá'   to fall flat on one's
                                   face accidentally

The actor focus verbal affix indicating the distributive is mang-. Mang- has a special use indicating plurality or distributiveness of action or habitual, repeated action.

Example

mang- + isda → mangisda   to fish (repetitively)

Mag- differs from mang- in that it has only a single action directed toward a single object while mang- usually indicates a habitual or professional action directed toward a multitude of objects.[1]

The actor focus verbal affix indicating the aptative is maka-. The maka- affix indicates ability to undergo the action named by the verb root. Similar to the ma- verb, it usually indicates a state of being rather than the dynamic nature of the mag-/-um- affixes.

Example

Nakakasayaw
Nakasasayaw   ako.   I can dance; I have the ability to dance.

Nagsasayaw
Sumasayaw   ako.   I am dancing.

However, when the last syllable of the affix is stressed, the meaning of involuntary action or acciden- tal action replaces the abilitative function of the affix.

Example

Base: káin   to eat

Nakakáin ako ng balut.   I was able to eat balut.

Nakákain ako ng balut.   I (unintentionally) ate balut.

Usually when the indicative verb form is a mag- verb, the abilitative affix form is makapag-.

Example

Indicative verb: maglabá   to wash (clothes)

Nakapaglaba ako ng damit kahapon.   I was able to wash clothes yesterday.

The actor focus verbal affix indicating a social action is maki-. The maki- affix is often used with the verb base, to request permission to use or partake of something or share that which is owned by another.

---

[1]Wolfenden, Elmer. A Re-statement of Tagalog Grammar. Institute of National Language, Manila, 1961.

Or it may make the verb base a request.

<u>Example</u>

Request: Makikuha ka nga ng   Please get me some
          tubig.   water.

Permission: Makitawag nga sa   May I use your
            telepono ninyo.   phone?

The actor focus verbal affix indicating the causative is <u>magpa</u>-. The <u>pa</u>- affix added to <u>mag</u>- means 'to cause, let, make, allow, or have' the action of the verb stem accomplished (done). Oftentimes a third person is involved in the sentence as the actor of the action. <u>Pa</u>- in this case means 'to cause or have somebody do something'. Besides <u>mag</u>-, the causative affix <u>pa</u>- can be combined with the abilitative affix <u>maka</u>-: Nakapagawa siya ng bahay. 'He was able to cause a house built.'

3.12 Goal Focus Affixes

The goal focus affixes point to the object or the goal as the topic of the sentence.

The indicative goal focus affixes follow.

(1) The -<u>in</u> suffix usually functions as the affix that focuses attention on the object of the sentence. Verbs that take this affix are called -<u>in</u> verbs. In most cases these -<u>in</u> verbs can be traced as the goal focus counterpart of the actor focus -<u>um</u>- verbs.

<u>Example</u>

Types of Verbs	Verb	Actor	Object
<u>Um</u>- verb	Bumili	<u>ka</u>	ng tinapay.
	'Buy	you	(some) bread.'
-<u>In</u> verb	Bilhin	mọ	<u>ang tinapay</u>.
	'Buy	you	the bread.'

(2) Some i- verbs also focus on the noun phrase complement that functions as the goal of the sentence. Unlike the -in verb, however, which usually requires a static, 'receiver-of-the-action' type of object, the i- verb goal undergoes the action stated by the verb. It is somewhat an 'instrumental goal'. The i- verb usually has a mag- verb counterpart rather than an -um- verb.

Example

Type of Verb	Verb	Actor	Object
Mag- verb	Magtapon 'Throw	ka you	ng basura. (indef.) garbage.'
I- verb	Itapon 'Throw	mo you	ang basura. the garbage.'

(3) In a few cases, -an may mark a topic as having the function of a goal. The -an affix is often considered a locative focus affix. Unlike the -in and the i- goal focus affixes, the -an goal focus affix occurs with a goal often associated with an area or surface. Its actor focus counterpart is often a mag- verb.

Example

Mag- Verb	-An Verb
Actor Focused	Goal Focused
Maglaba ka ng damit. (object)	Labhan mo ang damit.
'Wash the clothes.'	'Wash the clothes.'

The distributive goal focus affix is pang--in. Its actor focus counterpart is the mang- affix.

Example

Manghuli ka ng mga manok.   Catch some chickens.

Panghulihin mo ang mga manok. Catch the chickens.

The aptative goal focus affix is <u>ma</u>-. Its actor focus counterpart is <u>maka</u>-. Like <u>maka</u>- it has an accidental, unintentional meaning when the affix is stressed.

<u>Example</u>

Ability:	Nakáin niya ang balut.	He was able to eat the <u>balut</u>.
Accidental:	Nákain niya ang balut.	He (unintentionally) ate the <u>balut</u>.

The social goal focus affix is <u>paki</u>- and has its counterpart in the actor focus <u>maki</u>- verb. Unlike <u>maki</u>-, <u>paki</u>- is used more in requests.

<u>Example</u>

Paki-abot nga ang suka.	Please pass the vinegar.

The causative goal focus affix has two forms.

(1) <u>Ipa</u>- is the most common causative goal focus affix.

<u>Examples</u>

Ipatapon mo ang basura.	Have someone throw the garbage.
Ipatahi mo ang tela.	Have someone sew the cloth.

(2) <u>Pa--an</u> is used as a causative goal focus affix when the indicative goal focus affix is -<u>an</u>. <u>Ipa</u>-, however, can also be used in this case.

<u>Examples</u>

Palaban mo ang damit. (From: lab<u>an</u>)	(Also, <u>Ipalaba</u>)	Have someone wash the clothes.
Pabuksan mo ang pinto. (From: buks<u>an</u>)	(Also, <u>Ipabukas</u>)	Have someone open the door.

3.13 Locative Focus Affixes

The locative focus affixes point to the place or location as the topic of the sentence.

The indicative locative focus affixes are as follows.

(1) The -an suffix usually functions as the affix that focuses attention on the person or object or place toward which the action is directed or where the action is being carried out. Usually the actor focus counterpart of the -an suffix is -um-.

Example

	Verb	Actor	Location

Actor Focus
  -Um- Verb   Bumili   kami   sa kaniya.
                 'We bought from her.'
Locative Focus
  -An Verb   Binilhan namin siya.
                 'We bought from her.'

-An after vowel sounds becomes -han: bili + -an → bilihan. In rapid speech the unstressed i is dropped: bilhán.

(2) The pag--an compound affix also functions as a locative focus affix. It generally has the mag- affix as its actor focus counterpart.

Example

Verb	Actor	Location	
Nagluto	siya	sa palayok.	She cooked in
Pinaglutuan	niya	ang palayok.	the pot.

The pag--an affix focuses more on the place or the object where the action takes place rather than on the person.

The distributive locative focus affix is the pang--an compound affix often reduced to -an.

64

Example

Panghiraman⎤
Hiraman ⎦ ninyo sila ng silya.   (You) (pl)
                                    borrow chairs
                                    from them.

The aptative locative focus affix has two forms.

(1) The ma--an compound affix is the abilitative
locative focus affix of maka- verbs: Nahiraman niya ng
pera ang Nanay. 'He was able to borrow some money from
Mother.'

(2) The mapag--an compound affix is the locative
focus affix of makapag- verbs: Napaglutuan niya ng
ulam ang maliit na palayok. 'He was able to cook some
food in the small pot.'

The social locative focus affix is paki--an which
corresponds to the social verb, maki-: Pakitawagan mo
ang telepono nila. 'Please call by using their
telephone.'

The causative locative focus affix is pa--an:
Pabilhan mo ng tinapay ang tindahan nila. 'Make/Have
(someone) buy bread from their store.'

3.14 Benefactive Focus Affixes

The benefactive focus affixes point to the beneficiary as the topic of the sentence.

The indicative benefactive focus affixes have two
forms.

(1) The ipag- affix often focuses on the benefactive
complement (usually an animate noun for which the action
is performed). Its actor focus counterpart is usually
the mag- affix.

Example

Maglaba ka ng damit para   Wash the clothes for
   sa kaniya.   her.

Ipaglaba mo siya ng   Wash the clothes for
   damit.   her.

(2) The i- affix also focuses on the benefactive complement but its actor focus counterpart is usually the -um- affix.

Example

Bumili ka ng sapatos   Buy (you) shoes for me.
para sa akin.

Ibili mo ako ng sapatos.   Buy shoes for me.

The distributive benefactive focus affix is ipang-: Ipanghiram mo siya ng pera. 'Borrow some money for her.'

The aptative benefactive focus affixes have two forms.

(1) Ma- added to the i- benefactive affix makes up the abilitative benefactive focus affix counterpart of the maka- actor focus affix: Naibili ko siya ng baro. 'I was able to buy her a dress.'

(2) Ma- + i- + pag- is the benefactive focus affix of makapag-: Naipaglaba ko ang Nanay sa ilog. 'I was able to wash clothes for Mother at the river.'

The social benefactive focus affix is i- + paki-: Ipakibili mo siya ng gulay sa palengke. '(please) Buy some vegetables for her at the market.'

The causative benefactive focus affix has two forms.

(1) Ipa- is used as the usual causative benefactive focus affix. The form is similar to the causative goal focus affix: Ipabili mo ako ng yelo sa tindahan. 'Have somebody buy me some ice at the store.'

(2) Ipag- + pa- (-an) is used when the source is a mag-/-an verb: Ipagpalabhan/Ipagpalaba mo siya ng damit. 'Have someone wash the clothes for her.'

3.15 Instrumental Focus Affixes

The instrumental focus affixes point to the tool or the instrument used as the topic of the sentence.

The indicative instrumental focus affix is <u>ipang</u>-.
Oftentimes, <u>ipang</u>- is abbreviated to <u>i</u>- and is therefore
confused with the <u>i</u>- goal focus affix and the <u>i</u>-
benefactive focus affix. This affix is rarely used in
the language: Ipinangbalot ko sa libro ang diyaryo.
'I wrapped the book with the newspaper.'

The distributive instrumental focus affix is also
<u>ipang</u>-: Ipanghiram mo sa bangko ang titulo ng bahay mo.
'Use your title to your house to borrow money from the
bank.'

The aptative instrumental focus affix is <u>ma</u>- +
<u>ipang</u>-: Naipangbasa niya ng dyaryo ang aking salamin.
'He was able to read the newspapers with my eyeglasses.'

The social instrumental focus affix is <u>i</u>- + <u>paki</u>- +
<u>pang</u>-, a compound affix: Ipakipangbalot mo nga ng libro
ang papel. '(Please) use the paper to wrap the book.'

The causative instrumental focus affix is <u>ipa</u>- +
<u>pang</u>-. Usually this compound form is reduced to just
<u>ipang</u>-: Ipapangbalot mo ang papel sa libro. 'Have the
book wrapped with the paper.'

3.16 Aptative Causative Focus Affixes

The causative <u>pa</u>- affix can combine not only with
the indicative <u>mag</u>- but also with the aptative <u>maka</u>-.
This combination can be called the aptative causative.
Note the following.

AF	Nakapagawa Nakapagpagawa ⎤ ako ng bahay.	I was able to have a house built.
GF	Napagawa ko ang bahay.	I was able to have <u>the house</u> built.
BF	Naipagawa Naipagpagawa ⎤ ko siya ng bahay.	I was able to build a house for <u>her</u>.
LF	Napagawan Napagpagawan ⎤ ko ng bahay ang lupa ko.	I was able to have a house built on <u>my lot</u>.

IF Naipangpagawa ko ang naipon   I was able to have a
    kong pera.   house built <u>with</u>
                                        <u>the money I saved</u>.

     A combination of the aptative and the causative
also indicates either a very polite or indirect way
of requesting or describing an action, or implies that
it is possible to get someone to do something:[1]
Makapagpabili na nga sa iyo ng bigas. 'May I please
request you to buy me some rice.'

---

    [1]McKaughan, Howard. <u>Inflection</u> <u>and</u> <u>Syntax</u> <u>of</u>
<u>Maranao</u> <u>Verbs</u>. Institute of National Language, Manila,
1958. p. xiii.

SUMMARY AFFIX CHART

KIND OF ACTION	Actor	FOCUS				
		Goal	Benefactive	Locative	Instrumental	
Indicative	UM-	-in	i-	-an	ipang-	
	MAG-	-in	ipag-	-an	ipang-	
		-an	ipag-	pag--an	ipang-	
		i-	ipag-	-an	ipang-	
	MA-			-an	ipang-	
Distribu-tive	MANG-	pang--in -in	ipang-	pang--an	ipang-	
Aptative	MAKA-	ma-	ma+i-	ma--an	ma+i+pang-	
	MAKAPAG-	ma--an ma+i-	ma+i+pag-	ma+pag--an	ma+i+pang-	
Social	MAKI-	paki-	i+paki-	paki--an	i+paki+pang-	
Causative	MAGPA-	ipa- pa--an	ipa- ipag+pa-	pa--an pag+pa--an	ipa+pang- ipa+pang-	
Aptative Causative	MAKA+pa- MAKA+pag+pa-	ma+pa-	ma+i+pa- ma+i+pag+pa-	ma+pa--an ma+pag+pa--an	ma+i+pang+pa-	

SAMPLE WORD CHART WITH THE AFFIXES

KIND OF ACTION	FOCUS				
	Actor	Goal	Benefactive	Locative	Instrumental
Indicative	bumili	bilin	ibili	bilhan	ipangbili
	maglinis	linisin	ipaglinis	linisan	ipanglinis
	maglaba	labhan	ipaglaba	paglabhan	ipanglaba
	magtapon	itapon	ipagtapon	tapunan	ipangtapon
	matulog	--	--	tulugan	ipangtulog
Distributive	manghuli	panghulihin hulihin	ipanghuli	panghulihan	ipanghuli
Aptative	makabili	mabili	maibili	mabilhan	maipangbili
	makapaglaba	malaban	maipaglaba	mapaglabhan	maipanglaba
	makapagtapon	maitapon	maipagtapon	mapagtapunan	maipangtapon
Social	makitawag	pakitawag	ipakitawag	pakitawagan	ipakipangtawag
Causative	magpakuha	ipakuha	ipakuha	pakunan	ipapangkuha
	magpalaba	palaban	ipagpalaba	pagpalabhan	ipapanglaba
Aptative Causative	makapagpagawa	mapagawa	maipagpagawa	mapagawan	maipangpagawa
	makapagpagawa	mapagpagawa	maipagpagawa	mapagpagawan	

3.2 Major Affixes Used in the Formation of Adjectives or Descriptives

The unstressed prefix ma- when affixed to a descriptive root word, gives the word described the quality of that root word.

Examples

Root Word		Descriptive Word	
gandá	beauty	ma-gandá	beautiful
baít	goodness	ma-baít	good

When immediately followed by a noun, the linker (or ligature) -ng/na is added to the descriptive word.

Examples

maganda + babae → magandang babae 'beautiful woman'

mabait + bata → mabait na bata 'good child'

-An when added to certain root words denotes excessiveness or abundance.

Examples

dugó'	blood	duguán	bloody
pangá	jaw	pangahán	having a large jaw

When added to colors the function of this affix is similar to the -ish in English meaning 'like' or 'similar'.

Examples

pulá	red	pulahán	reddish
putí'	white	putián	whitish
abú	gray	abuhán (also abuhín)	grayish

(Note the use of -han after vowel sounds.)

Ka- denotes that the root word it is attached to
is of the 'same quality'.

Examples

| kúlay | color | kakúlay | of the same color |
| láhi' | race | kaláhi' | of the same race |

Maka- signifies 'inclination towards', 'in sympathy
with', 'in favor of' the quality expressed by the root
word.

Examples

lúma'	old	makalúma'	old-fashioned
báyan	country	makabáyan	patriotic
lúpa'	earth	makalúpa'	earthly, mundane

Pala- (or mapag-) indicates 'inclination towards',
'frequency of' or 'habitual action' as expressed by the
root word.

Examples

bíro'	joke	palabiró'	fond of jesting
káin	eat	palakaín	always eating
tanóng	ask ques- tions	palatanóng	always asking questions, inquisitive
túlog	sleep	palatulóg	always sleeping

Note the shift in stress in the pala- forms when
the roots have penultimate (second to the last syllable)
stress.

In many roots, without the prefix pala-, the
shifting of the stress of the root from penultimate to
ultimate syllable results in the change of the root
into an adjective.

Examples

| bíhis | way of dressing | bihís | dressed up |

bútas	hole	butás	punctured
bílang	number	biláng	counted
báli'	fracture	balí'	fractured

Pang- expresses utility or the purpose denoted by the root word.

Examples

pam-babae	for women's use (only)
pang-gabi	for use only during nighttime; works at night; night shift
pambahay	for use only in the house
panlalake	for men's use (only)

Note the changes of -ng to m and n before consonants b and d. These are morphophonemic changes.

Naka- plus noun, adjective or verb root is used as a modifier.

Examples

ang dalagang, nakakimona...	the girl, wearing a kimona (native blouse)...
ang taong, nakatayo sa kanto...	the man, standing at the corner...
ang babaing nakaluksa...	the woman who is in mourning...

3.3 Major Affixes Used in the Formation of Nouns or Substantives

-An is often used to form names of places as indicated by the root word.

Examples

aklát	book	aklátan	library
tindá	to sell	tindáhan	store
húgas	to wash	hugasán	place for washing

(Note the use of -han after vowel sounds.)

-An is also used to designate the instrument or means for realizing the action denoted by the root word.

Examples

| lúto' | to cook | lutuán | vessel for cooking |
| káin | to eat | kainán | vessel or place for eating |

-In- expresses the process by which a product has been produced.

Examples

sáing	to boil (rice)	sináing	boiled rice
íhaw	to roast	iníhaw	roasted
tápa	to slice thinly (as meat)	tinápa	(meat) sliced thinly
príto	to fry	piniríto	fried

Ka--an when affixed to a root word expresses abstract ideas.

Examples

ligaya	happy	kaligayahan	happiness
payapa'	peaceful	kapayapaan	peace
pangit	ugly	kapangitan	ugliness

Note that -an becomes -han when suffixed to a vowel sound.

Mag- denotes blood or social interrelationship when affixed to kinship terms.

Examples

| ina | mother | mag-ina | mother and child |
| asawa | spouse | mag-asawa | husband and wife |

With the first syllable of the root word reduplicated, the affix mag- also expresses occupation or
profession.

Examples

bóte	bottle	magboboté	one who collects and sells empty bottles for a living
nákaw	to steal	magnanákaw	thief, robber

Pag- is generally used to nominalize verbs. The
pag- stem is similar to the English gerund.

Examples

(-um-) inom	to drink	pag-inom	drinking
(-um-) basa	to read	pagbasa	reading

Pag- when attached to the root of a mag- verb
usually results in the reduplication of the first
syllable (CV-/V-) of the root.

Examples

(mag)basá	to read	pag-ba-basá	reading
(mag)labá	to wash (clothes)	pag-la-labá	washing (clothes)

Pang- expresses the instrument used for performing
what the root word denotes.

Examples

bútas	hole	pambútas	instrument used for boring holes
híwa'	to cut	panghíwa'	instrument used for cutting
púnas	to wipe	pamúnas	instrument used for wiping

When pang- is affixed to root words starting with
p-, b-, or m-, the final -ng of pang- becomes m-:
pang + bútas → pambútas.

When attached to root words starting with t-, d-,
or n-, the final -ng becomes n-: pang + damó → pandamó.

When prefixed to root words starting with g-, ng-,
or h-, and vowel sounds, the -ng of pang- remains un-
changed: pang + híwa → panghíwa'.

Taga- before verb roots means 'one whose occupation
or work is the one expressed by the verb'.

Examples

| makinílya | to type | taga-makinílya | typist |
| húkay | to dig | tagahúkay | digger |

If prefixed to place nouns, it signifies a native
or resident of a town, province, or country.

Examples

| taga-Mayníla' | from Manila, a resident of Manila |
| taga-Amérika | a native of America, an American |

The stressed affix máng-, prefixed to the root
plus a reduplication of the second syllable of the
stem (after the assimilation and loss of the initial
consonant of the root have taken place), indicates
occupation or a habitual kind of work.

Examples

Affix + Root	Assimilation	Reduplication of the second syllable
mang- + sayáw 'dance'	→ manayaw	→ mánanayaw 'dancer'
+ kulót 'curl'	→ mangulot	→ mángungulot 'beautician'

+ ʼisdá'	→ maṉgisda'	→ máṉgiṉgisda'	
'fish'		'fisherman'	
+ ṯahí'	→ maṉahi'	→ máṉaṉahi'	
'sew'		'seamstress'	
+ bilí	→ mamili	→ mámiṃili	
'buy'		'customer, buyer'	

When the initial consonant of the base is not lost
like h-, g-, and occasionally k-, the first CV- of the
root is reduplicated.

Examples

mang- + húla'	→ máṉghuhula'	prophet,	
'prediction'		seer	
+ gamót	→ máṉgagamot	doctor	
'medicine, cure'			
+ kúlam	→ máṉgkukulam	witch	
'witchcraft'			

Sometimes the -ng of mang- is modified according to
the point of articulation of the initial consonant of
the root (d-, l-).

Examples

mang- + dula'	→ maṉdula	→ mandudula'	playwright,
'drama, play'			dramatist
+ lakbay	→ maṉlakbay	→ manlalakbay	traveler
'travel'			

(Note that the first CV- of the root is reduplicated too.)

Ka- or ka--an denotes some affinity or direct
relationship.

Examples

túlong	help	katúlong	helper
sayáw	dance	kasayáw	dancing
			partner

áway	fight	kaáway	enemy
tabí	side	katabí	seatmate
sintá	loved one	kasintáhan	sweetheart
íbig	like, want	kaibígan	friend
báyan	country	kababáyan	countrymen (+ reduplication of CV- of root)
báta'	child	kababáta'	childhood friend

III. BASIC SENTENCE CONSTRUCTION

1. General

There are two types of Tagalog sentences: the Predicational and the Identificational.[1]

The Predicational sentence type has the comment (or predicate) before the topic (or subject), whereas the Identificational type has the topic occurring before the comment.

```
Predicational:     Tumakbo ang bata.
                   (comment) (topic)
                   'ran'    'the child'

Identificational:  Ang bata ang tumakbo.
                   (topic)   (comment)
                   'It was the child who ran.'
```

The predicational sentence has a definite topic marked by ang before common nouns or si before personal proper nouns.

Amerikano si Jorge.	George is an American.
Nasa bahay sina Carmen.	Carmen (and her companions) are in the house.

---

[1]Some grammarians call this type equational.

Maganda _ang_ babae.	The woman is beautiful.
Nag-aral _ang mga_ estudyante.	The students studied.

Ang- pronouns or _ang-_ demonstratives may substitute for the topic.

Amerikano _siya_.	He is an American.
Maganda _ito_.	This is beautiful.

The identificational sentence has two types: the definite and the indefinite.

The definite sentence type has a topic marked by either _ang_ or _si_ and a comment marked only by _ang_.[1]

Marked Topic (Definite)	Marked Comment (Definite)
Ang kriminal '(It was) the criminal	_ang_ pumatay. who killed.'
_Si_ Dick McGinn 'Dick McGinn	_ang_ direktor. (is) the director.'
Siya 'She	_ang_ maganda. (is) the beautiful (one).'
Ito 'This	_ang_ nasa bahay. (is what is) in the house.'

The indefinite sentence type has an unmarked topic (indefinite) and a marked comment (definite).

---

[1] An exception to this rule is when a personal pronoun or a demonstrative occurs in the topic position followed by a _si_ phrase identifying the topic.

Topic	Comment	
Ako	si Pedro.	I am Pedro.
Siya	si Binibining Paz.	She is Miss Paz.
Ito	si Ginoong Cruz.	This is Mr. Cruz.

This type of sentence is commonly used in introductions.

Unmarked Topic (Indefinite)	Marked Comment (Definite)
Kriminal '(A) criminal	ang pumatay. was the one who killed.'
Bata '(A) child	ang tumakbo. was the one who ran.'
Pulis '(A) policeman	ang matapang. was the strong one.'
Santos 'Santos	ang pangalan niya. was his name.'

2. Construction of a Predicational Sentence

The most common sentence is the Predicational type. A Tagalog predicational sentence consists of at least two major grammatical constituents or parts: the Topic (or what is usually referred to as the 'subject' in an English sentence) and the Comment which is similar to the 'predicate' in function.

The regular order of these two basic elements is as follows:

Comment + Topic

(Predicate) (Subject)

In an English sentence the regular arrangement of the two major grammatical elements is the opposite:

Subject + Predicate

2.1 The Topic

The topic (or subject) may be either a non-verbal or a verbal phrase.

The non-verbal topic of a sentence is a noun or a noun phrase (a noun with its attributes) introduced by the focus-marking particles ang or si. Ang precedes common nouns such as babae 'woman', bata 'child', etc. Si is followed by proper nouns such as Pedro, Maria, etc. The ang phrase or si phrase can be replaced by the ako set of pronouns or the ito set of demonstratives.

Henceforth, the ako set of pronouns, the ito set of
demonstratives and the ang/si marked noun phrases will
be referred to as the ang pronouns, the ang demonstratives, and the ang phrases respectively.

The following give examples of the ang phrases and
their substitutes.

(1) Ang phrases.

Number	Si + Proper Noun	Ang + Common Noun
Singular	si Pedro 'Pedro'	ang lapis 'the pencil'
Plural	sina Pedro 'Pedro and his companions'	ang (mga)[1] lapis 'the pencils'

(2) Ang pronouns.

Number	Person	Ang Pronoun	Gloss
Singular	1	ako	I
	1-2 (dual)	kata[2]	you and I
	2	ikaw/ka	you
	3	siya	he/she
Plural	1 (excl)	kami	we (I and others)
	1-2 (incl)	tayo	we (I, you and others)
	2	kayo	you (pl)
	3	sila	they

---

[1] Mga as a plural marker is optional.

[2] The use of kata is regional now.

(3) <u>Ang</u> demonstratives.

Number	Ang Demonstrative	Gloss
Singular	ito/iri[1]	this one (here)
	iyan	that one (far)
	iyon	that one (yonder)
Plural	ang mga ito/iri	these ones (here)
	ang mga iyan	those ones (far)
	ang mga iyon	those ones (yonder)

The <u>topic</u> is any noun phrase complement which is the focus of attention in the sentence. It can be the doer, the object, the beneficiary, the instrument, or the location of the action.

A non-verbal topic phrase has basically a noun preceded by <u>ang</u>. However <u>ang</u> may also precede an adjective, a prepositional phrase, an existential phrase or an adverbial phrase. In each case the entire construction including <u>ang</u> is the topic. The following illustrate with the topic underlined.

(1) Nominal Phrase

    Common Pronoun Demonstrative

        Tumakbo <u>ang bata</u>.   <u>The child</u> ran.

        Tumakbo <u>siya</u>.   <u>He</u> ran.

        Tumakbo <u>ito</u>.   <u>This (one)</u> ran.

    Proper

        Nasa bayan <u>si Pedro</u>.   <u>Pedro</u> is in town.

(2) Adjectival Phrase

    Nanalo <u>ang maganda</u>.   <u>The beautiful (one)</u> won.

    Walang anak <u>ang mayaman</u>.   <u>The rich (one)</u> (is) childless.

---

[1] <u>Iri</u> is a regional variant of <u>ito</u>.

(3) Prepositional Phrase

Sa phrase

Primera premyo <u>ang sa Maynila</u>.	<u>The (one) for Manila</u> (is the) first prize.

Nasa phrase

Nawala <u>ang nasa kaniya</u>.	<u>That (which is) with him/in his possession</u> got lost.

Para sa phrase

Nahulog <u>ang para sa bata'</u>.	<u>The (one) for the child</u> fell/dropped.

(4) Existential Phrase

Maganda <u>ang may asawa</u>.	<u>The married (one is)</u> beautiful.

(5) Adverbial Phrase

Adverb of time

Parada <u>ang bukas</u>.	<u>The (one for) tomorrow</u> (is a) parade.

Adverb of manner

Mas mabuti <u>ang patagilid</u>.	<u>That (position which is) on the side</u> is better.

The topic of a predicational sentence can be a verb preceded by <u>ang</u>. This marked verbal form is nominalized and usually constitutes the topic of the sentence unless there is another <u>ang</u> construction or an <u>ang</u> pronoun in the sentence in which case the <u>ang</u> verbal phrase then becomes the definite comment.

Note the following examples.

Mahirap <u>ang magluto'</u>.	It is difficult <u>to cook</u>.

Madali <u>ang kumain</u>.　　　It is easy <u>to eat</u>.

Masarap <u>ang matulog</u>.　　It is nice <u>to sleep</u>.

In rapid speech, the topic marker <u>ang</u> is often dropped except where the comment ends with a vowel like <u>madali</u> in which case <u>ang</u> is contracted to -<u>ng</u> and attached to the word:　Madali<u>ng</u> kumain pero mahirap magluto'.　'It is easy to eat but difficult to cook.'

Further examples follow.

Nalunod <u>ang lumalangoy</u>.　　<u>The one swimming</u> drowned.

Kumakanta <u>ang nagtatrabaho</u>.　<u>The ones working</u> are singing.

Humihilik <u>ang natutulog</u>.　　<u>The one sleeping</u> is snoring.

Nahuli <u>ang nagnakaw</u>.　　<u>The one who stole (something)</u> was caught.

2.2　The Comment

The <u>comment</u> (or predicate) of a predicational sentence may be either a non-verbal or a verbal phrase.

2.21　Non-verbal Phrases

Non-verbal phrases include a nominal phrase, an adjectival phrase, a prepositional phrase, an adverbial phrase or an existential phrase (phrase introduced by existential particles <u>may</u>/<u>mayroon</u>).　These non-verbal phrases are descriptive in nature.

These phrases occurring in the comment position (before the <u>ang</u> phrase) are illustrated in the following sentences.

(1) Nominal phrase comment

<u>Doktor</u> ang lalake.　　The man is a doctor.

<u>Pebrero</u> ang kaarawan ko.　　My birthday is in February.

(2) Adjectival phrase comment

Payat ang bata.	The child is thin.
Pangit ang dalaga.	The unmarried woman is ugly.
Maganda ang bahay.	The house is beautiful.
Matalino ang guro'.	The teacher is intelligent.
Mahirap ang magturo'.	Teaching is difficult.

(3) Prepositional phrases as comment

a. With sa and the sa pronouns (specifying location)

Sa atin ⎤				our ⎤	
Sa inyo	ang handa.	The party is at	your	place.
Sa amin				our (excl)	
Sa kanila ⎦				their ⎦	

If personal proper nouns are used to indicate location, kina is used before the name. Kina is the plural form of kay: Kina Joy ang handa. 'The party is at Joy's (place) or at Joy's (and her family's place).'

The demonstrative pronouns that can replace locative phrases marked by sa are dito, diyan and doon. They are referred to as sa demonstratives.

Dito ⎤				here. ⎤
Diyan	ang parada.	The parade is	there.
Doon ⎦			over there. ⎦

Sa pronouns also indicate possession. The sa marker before the sa pronouns however is not obligatory in this position. These forms may appear in the topic position as follows:

Akin ang lapis.	The pencil is mine.
Iyo ang kotse.	The car is yours.
Kanila ang tindahan.	The store is theirs.

Kay and kina before proper nouns are also used to indicate possession: Kay Lina ang belo. 'The veil is Lina's.' Kina Jose ang pagkain. 'The food is Jose's and his companions.'

b. With nasa (definite position or location of objects that are usually small or movable)

Nasa sala ang piyano.	The piano is in the living room.
Nasa mesa ang pambura.	The eraser is on the table.
Nasa bahay ang plantsa.	The flat iron is in the house.
Nasa opisina ang makinilya.	The typewriter is in the office.

The nasa constructions may also express possession of the topic.

Nasa akin			my possession.
Nakay Fe	ang lapis.		Fe's possession.
Nakina Juan		The pencil is in	Juan and his company's possession.
Nasa estudyante			the student's possession.

Like the sa pronouns, the sa demonstratives can also take na-. The combination results in the forms nandito, nandiyan, nandoon with the variant forms narito, nariyan, and naroon, respectively. Both forms are commonly used.

Nandito (Narito)			here.
Nandiyan (Nariyan)	ang sasakyan.	The vehicle is	there
Nandoon (Naroon)			over there.

c. With para sa (benefactive comments)

Para sa bisita ⎤
Para sa kaniya ⎬ ang pagkain. The food is ⎡ for the
Para dito ⎦   visitor
                                                for him.
                                                for this
                                                (place).

    Kay/kina replaces sa in para sa when what follows
is a personal proper noun.

Para kay Loida ⎤   ⎡ for Loida.
Para kina Cres ⎦ ang regalo. The gift is ⎨ for Cres
                                                and her
                                                companions.

    Thus the para sa phrase expresses that its topic
(usually an object) is for somebody, for something, or
for some place.

Para sa bata ang kendi.   The candy is for the
                              child.

Para kay Ben ang pitaka'.   The wallet is for Ben.

Para sa iyo ang sinturon.   The belt is for you.

Para diyan ito.   This is for that.

Para sa mesa ang tapete.   This tablecloth is for
                              the table.

    d. With the existential phrases (the existence or
the possession of something--may/mayroon 'there is';
wala, non-existence)

    The sentences below give only the possessive
function of the existential phrase. The existential
function of may/mayroon is illustrated under topicless
sentences.

May asawa ang babae.   The woman has a spouse.

May aso ako.   I have a dog.

Mayroong asawa si   Mang Juan has a spouse.
  Mang Juan.

Mayroong bahay sila.	They have a house.
Walang asawa ang guro ko.	My teacher has no spouse.
Walang pera ang nanay.	Mother has no money.

Note that both <u>mayroon</u> and <u>wala</u> take a linker before an immediately following object. <u>May</u> does not. Either <u>mayroon</u> or <u>wala</u> can stand alone as a single-word response but not <u>may</u>.

Unlike <u>mayroon</u>, <u>may</u> is always followed immediately by the object word of whose existence or possession it is referring to. With <u>mayroon</u>, one can say <u>Mayroon kaming lapis</u> but never *<u>May kaming lapis</u>. It should be <u>May lapis kami</u>.

e. With adverbial phrases (time words or adverbs of manner)

Bukas ang parada.	The parade is tomorrow.
Ka-hapon ang suweldo.	Pay day was yesterday.
Sa linggo ang sabong.	Cockfighting will be on Sunday.
Noong Mayo ang Santa Cruzan.	The Santa Cruzan was last May.
Paluhod ang lakad niya.	He walked on his knees.
Patagilid ang tulog niya.	He slept on his side.

2.22 Verbal Phrases

A verbal phrase is composed of a verb with or without its attributes. A verb may co-occur with one or more complements. A complement is a noun phrase related to the verb as its actor, object, benefactor, location, or instrument.

Verbs as a grammatical category are differentiated from other parts of speech by their being marked for <u>focus</u> and <u>aspect</u>.

Focus

Focus refers to the grammatical relationship that
exists between the verb and one verbal complement
marked by the focus marker <u>ang</u>. This complement is
referred to as the <u>topic</u> of the sentence. The relationship of the topic to the verb may be: (1) the <u>actor</u>
who does or originates the action; (2) the <u>goal</u> which
is the object of the action; (3) the <u>locative</u> which is
the place of the action; (4) the <u>benefactive</u> who or
which is the beneficiary of the action; or (5) the
<u>instrument</u> which is the tool or means used to bring
about the action. The topic of the sentence may not
only be represented by the <u>ang</u> phrase but also by the
<u>ang</u> substitutes, either an <u>ang</u> pronoun or an <u>ang</u>
demonstrative. A verbal affix indicates one of these
relationships of the topic to the verb.

Focus may be viewed as referring to voice, except
that in Tagalog or in most Philippine languages, the
division would not be limited to the English active and
passive voices. The English active voice may be equated
to the Tagalog actor focus; the English passive voice
to the goal focus, but Tagalog adds three more focuses,
the locative, the benefactive, and the instrumental,
marked differently in the verb stem. Some linguists
analyzed Tagalog as having three or four sub-types in
the passive voice. In this grammar, <u>focus</u> will be used
instead of <u>voice</u> and five types of focus will be discussed. These five types of grammatical relationships
that exist between the verb and one focused verbal
complement (or <u>topic</u>) are marked, as indicated above, by
verbal affixes.

(1) Some verbal affixes that indicate that the
actor, doer, or the originator of the action is in
focus are -<u>um</u>-, <u>mag</u>-, <u>mang</u>-, <u>ma</u>-, and <u>maka</u>-. These may
be illustrated as follows.

Actor Focus	Verb	Topic (Actor)	Remainder	Gloss
-Um-:	Bumili	ang bata	ng tinapay.	The child bought some bread.

Mag-:	Magbili	ka	ng gulay.	(You) sell some vege- tables.
Mang-:	Nanghuli	ito	ng daga.	This (one) caught a rat.
Ma-:	Natulog	si Mila	kanina.	Mila slept a while ago.
Maka-:	Nakasa- sayaw Nakaka- sayaw	ako	ng "Pan- danggo sa Ilaw".	I can dance "Pandanggo sa Ilaw".
Makapag-:	Nakapag- luluto Nakaka- pagluto	siya	ng adobo.	She can cook "adobo".

(2) Verbal affixes that indicate that the topic of the sentence is the object or goal of the action include -in, i-, -an, and ma-. -In is commonly used as the characteristic goal focus marker.

Goal Focus	Verb	Actor	Topic (Goal)	Gloss
-in	Bilhin	mo	ang tinapay.	(You) buy the bread.
i-	Isulat	mo	ang kuwento.	(You) write the story.
-an	Labhan	mo	ang damit.	(You) wash the dress.
ma-	Nasasayaw	ko	ang Pandanggo.	I can dance the Pandanggo.

(3) The verbal affixes that indicate that the topic is the location of the action or the action is done toward that direction include -in, -an, and pag--an. In most cases -an is used for this focus.

Locative	Verb	Actor	Topic (Location)	Gloss
-an	Puntah<u>an</u>	mo	<u>ang bahay niya</u>.	(You) go to their house.
-in	Akyat<u>in</u>	mo	<u>ang bundok</u>.	(You) climb the mountain.
pag--an	<u>Pag</u>labh<u>an</u>	mo	<u>ang batya'</u>.	(You) wash the clothes in the basin.
mapag--an	<u>Napaglutuan</u>	ko	<u>ang palayok</u>.	I was able to cook in <u>the pot</u>.

(4) The verbal affixes that indicate that the topic is the beneficiary of the action are generally *i-* or *ipag-*. In a very few cases, *-an* is used.

Bene-factive	Verb	Actor	Topic (Beneficiary)	Goal	Gloss
i-	<u>I</u>bili	mo	<u>ang nanay</u>	ng sapatos.	(You) buy (a pair of) shoes (for) <u>Mother</u>.
ipag-	<u>Ipag</u>laba	mo	<u>ang maysakit</u>	ng damit.	(You) wash clothes (for) <u>the sick one</u>.
-an	Bilh<u>an</u>	mo	<u>ang bata</u>	ng sapatos.	(You) buy shoes (for) <u>the child</u>.

(5) The verbal affix that refers to anything used or acted upon to bring about the action as topic is *ipang-* usually shortened to *i-*.

Instru- mental	Verb	Actor	Topic (Instrument)	Gloss
ipang-	Ipanghiwa	mo	ang kutsilyo.	(You) use the knife to cut.
i(pang)-	Ipunas	mo	ang basahan.	(You) use the rag to wipe (something)
maipang-	Naipanglinis	ko	ang bangong walis.	I was able to use the new broom for cleaning.

Aspect

Tagalog verbs are inflected for aspect rather than tense as in English. Aspects indicate whether the action has started or not, and, if started, whether it has been completed or if it is still continuing. The three aspects are (1) completed, for action started and terminated, (2) contemplated, for action not started, and (3) incompleted, for action started but not yet completed or action still in progress. The form of the verb that is not inflected for aspect is neutral and may be called the infinitive form. The infinitive form of the verb is used for commands or imperatives.

The closest equivalents of the Tagalog aspects in English are the past, future, and progressive tenses to equate with completed, contemplated and incompleted respectively.

The processes involved in verbal inflection to indicate the different aspects differ according to the focus affix taken by the verb.

Actor focus verbs are inflected for aspect as follows.

The mag- affix is neutral as to aspect. Usually a simple replacement of m- by n- shows that an action has started.

Neutral:	maglaba	to wash (clothes)
Completed:	naglaba	washed (clothes)

When the action has started, a further distinction
is made as to whether it is still going on or it has
been completed. Partial reduplication (i.e., repetition
of one syllable of the word) signals continuation or
progress of the action as distinct from action that has
stopped or been completed.

> Continuous: nag-la-laba   washing (clothes)
>
> Completed: nag-laba   washed (clothes)

The contemplated aspect, because the action has
not started and is merely contemplated or anticipated,
retains the m- and the first syllable, CV- or V- of the
verb base is reduplicated to indicate the "incompleted-
ness" of the action.

> mag-li-linis   is cleaning
>
> mag-a-aral   is studying

Unlike the mag- affix, the -um- verb does not have
any overt marker or signal that indicates the completed
aspect. Its neutral or infinitive form is the same as
its completed form.

> Neutral: Tumula ako.   I recite a poem.
>
> Completed: Tumula ako.   I recited a poem.

The affix um- is placed before the first vowel
of the verb root or base, so it is an infix if the base
starts with a consonant, and a prefix if it starts with
a vowel.

> um- + langoy → l-um-angóy   to swim; swam
>
> um- + inom → um-inóm   to drink; drank

The um- affix is lost with the contemplated
(future) aspect. The first CV- (consonant-vowel) or V-
(if the base starts with a vowel) of the verb root is
reduplicated. This same type of reduplication with the
um- affix indicates the incompleted aspect. Note the
following.

a. Verb base: <u>basa</u> 'read'

Infinitive/Neutral	b-um-ása
Completed (past)	b-um-ása
Contemplated (future)	ba-bása
Incompleted (progressive)	b-um-a-bása

b. Verb base: <u>inom</u> 'drink'

Infinitive/Neutral	um-inóm
Completed (past)	um-inóm
Contemplated (future)	i-inóm
Incompleted (progressive)	um-i-inóm

The <u>ma-</u> verb aspect formation rules follow closely
the <u>mag-</u> verb aspect formation rules. Note the same
rules or processes of formation in the following
examples.

a. Verb base: <u>tulog</u> 'sleep'

Infinitive/Neutral	ma-túlog
Completed	na-túlog
Contemplated	ma-tu-túlog
Incompleted	na-tu-túlog

b. Verb base: <u>upo'</u> 'sit'

Infinitive	ma-upó'
Completed	na-upó'
Contemplated	ma-u-upó'
Incompleted	na-u-upó'

The <u>mang-</u> affix undergoes the same process as the
<u>mag-</u> and <u>ma-</u> affixes but there are some changes in the
final nasal sound of the affix as it is influenced by
the following initial sound of the root. These are
referred to as <u>morphophonemic</u> changes.

There is <u>partial assimilation</u> where the final nasal

sound /-ng/ of the affix is modified according to the point of articulation of the sound that immediately follows it. After the change of the /-ng/ to -m or -n, the first consonant of the root is dropped.

a. mang- + bili → mamilí   to buy

             pila → mamila   to choose

b. mang- + tahi'   → manahí'   to sew

           dalangin → manalángin   to pray

           sunog   → manúnog   to burn

c. mang- + kuha → mangúha   to get

          'isda → mangisdá'   to fish

Verb bases having initial consonants 1 and a few with d retain these sounds after the final /-ng/ of mang- has undergone the sound change:

mang- + likum → manlíkum   to collect

       damo → mandamó   to weed

The second syllable (first CV or V) of the affixed form that has undergone morphophonemic changes is reduplicated to indicate the incompleted forms of the verbs: mang- + bili → mamimili.

Some other forms with mang- follow.

Root	Neutral	Completed	Contemplated	Incompleted
mang- pili'	mamili'	namili'	mamimili'	namimili'
'to choose'				
mang- tahi'	manahi'	nanahi'	mananahi'	nananahi'
'to sew'				
mang- sunog	manunog	nanunog	manununog	nanununog
'to burn'				
mang- kuha	manguha	nanguha	mangunguha	nangunguha
'to get'				
mang- gulo	manggulo	nanggulo	manggugulo	nanggugulo
'to make trouble'				

mang-	likum manlikum 'to collect'	nanlikum	manlilikum	nanlilikum
mang-	damo mandamo 'to weed'	nandamo	mandadamo	nandadamo
mang-	isda' mangisda' 'to fish'	nangisda'	mangingisda'	nangingisda'
mang-	huli manghuli 'to catch (something)'	nanghuli	manghuhuli	nanghuhuli

The _maka-_ affix is inflected like the _ma-/mag-_
verbs except that in many cases, unexplainable by native
speakers, the last CV of the affix is reduplicated
rather than the first CV- or V- of the root. In other
cases, either one is acceptable.

Root: _sayaw_ 'to dance'

Aspect	Formulation	Example	Gloss
Neutral	maka + root	makasayaw	to be able to dance
Completed	naka + root	nakasayaw	was able to dance
Contemplated	$\begin{bmatrix} \text{maka} + C_1V_1 + \text{root} \\ \text{makaka} + \text{root} \end{bmatrix}$	$\begin{bmatrix} \text{makasasayaw} \\ \text{makakasayaw} \end{bmatrix}$	will be able to dance
Incompleted	$\begin{bmatrix} \text{naka} + C_1V_1 + \text{root} \\ \text{nakaka} + \text{root} \end{bmatrix}$	$\begin{bmatrix} \text{nakasasayaw} \\ \text{nakakasayaw} \end{bmatrix}$	being able to dance

To express involuntary or accidental action, the
affix receives an additional stress.

makabása	to be able to read (ability)
makábasa	to be able to read unintentionally (accidental)

Unlike the previous actor focus affixes, _maki-_
verbs only reduplicate the last syllable of the affix
instead of the first CV-/V- of the base for the contemplated and the incompleted aspects.

Verb base: <u>bili</u> 'to buy'

Infinitive   makibilí

Completed   nakibilí

Contemplated   makikibilí

Incompleted   nakikibilí

The non-actor focus verbs are inflected for aspect as follows.

The -<u>an</u> affix is always suffixed to the verb root. To indicate started action, -<u>in</u>- is affixed before the first vowel of the verb base.

Verb base: <u>punas</u> 'to wipe'

Neutral   punásan

Completed   pinunásan

Contemplated   pupunásan

Incompleted   pinupunásan

In most cases, the word base stress shifts to the next syllable after the -<u>an</u> is suffixed.

When the verb base ends in a vowel sound, -<u>an</u> becomes -<u>han</u>.

Verb base: <u>punta</u> 'to go'

Neutral   puntahán

Completed   pinuntahán

Contemplated   pupuntahán

Incompleted   pinupuntahán

The -<u>in</u> verb inflects for aspect the same way -<u>an</u> does, except that the -<u>in</u> suffix is dropped when the -<u>in</u>- to indicate started action occurs.

Verb base: <u>alis</u> 'to remove'

Neutral	alisín
Completed	inalís
Contemplated	aalisín
Incompleted	inaalís

Note that only when -<u>in</u> is suffixed to the root is there a shift of the word-base stress to the next syllable. Otherwise the stress remains in the same position as found in the root.

As in the -<u>an</u> verbs, when the verb base ends in a vowel sound, -<u>in</u> becomes -<u>hin</u>.

Verb base: <u>basa</u> 'to read'

Neutral	basahin
Completed	binasa
Contemplated	babasahin
Incompleted	binabasa

There are some word bases that drop their final unstressed vowels when the -<u>in</u>/-<u>an</u> form is suffixed to the root. The reduced form is more common in speech.

labá + an → labahán → labhán

bilí + in → bilihín → bilhín

dalá + in → dalahín → dalhín

gawá' + in → gawaín → gawín

Another modified form is exemplified by <u>kúha</u> + -<u>in</u> which by the regular process of change should have been <u>kúha</u> + -<u>hin</u>. However this form becomes <u>kúnin</u>.

Another irregular formation in colloquial use is <u>in</u>- with verb bases that begin with <u>l</u>-. In these cases the affix <u>in</u>- changes to <u>ni</u>- and is prefixed to the base to form the completed and incompleted aspects. It is only true for verb forms where the action has started. The other forms follow the regular process of change.

	Completed	Incompleted
in + lúto'	nilúto'	nilulúto'
in + línis	nilínis	nililínis
in + lága'	nilága'	nilalága'

However, in some parts of the Tagalog-speaking region, these verbs <u>luto'</u>, <u>laga'</u>, and <u>linis</u> follow the regular process of change in inflecting for aspect.

The <u>i-</u> affix is always prefixed to the root. The following chart shows the aspect formation of the <u>i-</u> verb.

Verb base: <u>abot</u> 'hand over'

Neutral	iabót
Completed	iniabót
Contemplated	iaabót
Incompleted	iniaabót

Note the metathesis or inversion of the affix <u>-in</u> to <u>ni-</u> when the verb base starts with a vowel. This is also true when the base starts with <u>h-</u> or <u>y-</u>, <u>n-</u> or <u>l-</u> (at least in most instances).

i + hatíd → inihatíd	inihahatíd
i + yári' → iniyári'	iniyayári'
i + nakaw → ininakaw	ininanakaw
i + linis → inilinis	inililinis

Verb base: <u>tápon</u> 'to throw'

Neutral	itápon
Completed	itinápon
Contemplated	itatápon
Incompleted	itinatápon

Note that <u>-in</u> does not change in form when infixed after the initial consonant of the verb root.

Ipag- verbs behave like the other verbs except that -in- the indicator of action started is infixed in the affix rather than in the verb root.

Verb base: <u>luto'</u> 'to cook'

Infinitive	ipaglúto'
Completed	ipinaglúto'
Contemplated	ipaglulúto'
Incompleted	ipinaglulúto'

The <u>ipang-</u> verb is inflected in the same manner as the <u>ipag-</u> verb. The only difference is that the final nasal sound of the affix undergoes the same morphophonemic changes undergone by the <u>mang-</u> affix.

ipang- + butas → ipambutas

Neutral	ipambutas
Completed	ipinambutas
Incompleted	ipinambubutas
Contemplated	ipambubutas

<u>Pang-</u> undergoes the same morphophonemic changes for the final nasal as does <u>mang-</u>.

<u>Pang--in</u> with the following bases illustrates.

Neutral	Completed	Contemplated	Incompleted
<u>pili'</u> 'to choose'			
pamilí'in	pinamilí'	pamimilí'in	pinamimíli'
<u>tahi</u> 'to sew'			
panahi'ín	pinanahí'	pananahi'ín	pinananahí
<u>kuha</u> 'to get'			
panguháin	pinangúha	pangunguháin	pinangungúha
<u>isda'</u> 'to fish'			
pangisda'ín	pinangisdá'	pangngingi-isda'ín	pinangingisdá'
<u>huli</u> 'to catch'			
panghulíhin	pinanghúli	panghuhulíhin	pinanghuhúli

Note the shift in stress to the next syllable when
a suffix is added to the verb stem. Note also the
absence of the suffix -in where the -in- signifying
action started is present.

The aspect formation of the abilitative or aptative
goal focus ma- verb is similar to the actor focus ma-
verb.

Verb base: kain 'eat'

Infinitive	makáin
Completed	nakáin
Contemplated	makakáin
Incompleted	nakakáin

Verb base: abót 'to hand over'

Infinitive	maabót
Completed	naabót
Contemplated	maaabót
Incompleted	naaabót

The prefix ma- is stressed when the action is
accidental or unintentional: madalá 'to be able to
carry'; mádala 'to carry by accident, or unintentionally'.

Paki-, like its actor focus counterpart maki-, is
reduplicated to indicate non-completed action.

Verb base: bili 'to buy'

Infinitive	pakibilí
Completed	pinakibilí
Contemplated	pakikibilí
Incompleted	pinakikibilí

2.3 The Complement

The topic is always in a focus relation to the
action expressed by the verbal predicate or comment.
Other noun phrases may be related to the verb as actor,

goal, benefactor, locator or instrument also, but not be in focus. These complements are composed of a non-focus particle plus a noun and its attributes, if any, or noun phrase substitutes.

When the verbal complement is not in focus, it is marked by particles ng, sa, or para sa indicating the grammatical function of the complement in the sentence.

In basic sentences, the actor, goal and instrumental complements are introduced by the marker ng and are called ng phrase complements. Examples of the ng phrases and their substitutes follow.

An actor complement is composed of the ng/ni marker followed by a common or proper noun or any of the appropriate phrase substitutes.

Binili⌈ng babae ang damit.   The woman⌉bought the dress.
     | niya   She |
     | nito   This (one) |
     ⌊ ni Maria   Maria   ⌋

A goal complement is composed of the marker ng/ni followed by either the common or proper noun or appropriate substitutes.

Bumili si Maria⌈ng damit.   Maria bought⌈a dress.
               ⌊nito.   ⌊this (one).

The goal complement does not admit personal proper nouns marked by ni/nina and ng pronouns. If the pronoun has to appear as the non-focused object of the sentence, it has to be a sa pronoun. The same is true for the personal noun. It has to be marked by kay/kina.

Goal Focus

Pinatay ni Luis⌈si Pedro.   Pedro⌉(was the one) killed
               ⌊siya.   He   ⌋   by Luis.

Goal Complement

Si Luis ang pumatay⌈kay Pedro.   Luis killed⌈Pedro.
                   ⌊sa kaniya.   ⌊him.

An instrumental complement is composed of the
marker ng/ni or the phrase sa pamamgitan ng/ni followed
by a common or proper noun or appropriate substitutes
for the phrase.

Binato niya ⌈ng unan ang bata.   He threw ⌈the pillow at the
          ⌊nito   ⌊it   child.

Note that the ng phrases above can be replaced by
ng pronouns and ng demonstratives.

In the preceding example note that the actor and
the goal are marked by ng when not in focus. By simply
looking at the marker one cannot tell which of the two
grammatical functions it has. This distinction however
is made clear by the verb stem. If the verb has an um-,
mag- or ma- affix, the focus is on the actor; hence,
the ng phrases that can occur with it will usually be
a goal. On the other hand, if the affix is -in, the
focus is on the goal and therefore the ng phrase that
occurs with it is the actor. Another ng phrase which
can also occur in a sentence with a goal topic is an
instrumental complement. Very often the semantic
feature of the noun (usually a tool, or the means to
bring about the action) following the marker ng suggests
its function in the sentence.

Examples of the ng phrase complements and its
pronoun and demonstrative substitutes follow.

(1) Ng phrases

Singular	ni Pedro		ng babae
	'of/by Pedro'		'of/by the woman'
Plural	nina Pedro		ng mga babae
	'of/by Pedro and		'of/by the women'
	his companions		
	(or and others)'		

(2) Ng forms of the personal pronouns

Singular	1	ko	of/by me; my _____
	2	mo	of/by you; your _____
	3	niya	of/by him/her; his/her _____

```
Plural      1    namin      of/by us; our (excl) _____
                 natin      of/by us; our (incl) _____
            2    ninyo      of/by you; your _____
            3    nila       of/by them; their _____
```

(3) <u>Ng</u> forms of the demonstrative pronouns

```
Singular    nire           of/by this (very near)
            nito           of/by this (near)
            niyan          of/by that (far)
            noon           of/by that (farther)

Plural      ng mga iri     of/by these (very near)
            ng mga ito     of/by these (near)
            ng mga iyan    of/by those (far)
            ng mga iyon    of/by those (farther)
```

A locative complement is composed of the <u>sa</u> marker plus a common or proper noun or any appropriate substitute for the phrase.

Pumunta ang mga tao <u>sa bayan</u>.
                                  <u>doon</u>.
                                  <u>kina Aling Maria</u>.
                                  <u>sa amin</u>.

'The people went to town.'
                            there.'
                            to Aling Maria's (place).'
                            to us (incl).'

Note again that <u>sa</u> pronouns and demonstratives can substitute for the <u>sa</u> phrases.

A benefactive complement is composed of the marker <u>para sa</u> plus a common or proper noun or any appropriate substitutes.

Bumili siya ng tinapay <u>para sa bata</u>.
                                      <u>kay Pedro</u>.
                                      <u>sa kaniya</u>.
                                      <u>sa bahay</u>.
                                      <u>dito</u>.

'He bought bread for the child.'
                        Pedro.'
                        him.'
                        the house.'
                        this (place).'

Again, note that <u>sa</u> phrases after <u>para</u> can be replaced by <u>sa</u> + <u>sa</u> pronouns or by <u>sa</u> demonstratives.

2.4 <u>Verbal Co-occurrence with Complements</u>

We have noted that verbs with focus affixes mark syntactic relations between the verb and its topic in the sentence. It should further be noted that there are co-occurrence restrictions between the verb stems and their syntactic complements. Verbs may be characterized by the privilege with which the basic complements can occur with them. Some complements are <u>obligatory</u> (required) with certain verbs, <u>optional</u> (may or may not occur) with others, and <u>absent</u> with others.

Depending on the focus as marked by the verbal affix, Tagalog verbs select the various complements which we have categorized as <u>actor complement</u>, <u>goal complement</u>, <u>locative complement</u>, <u>benefactive complement</u> and <u>instrumental complement</u>. Almost all sentences have one of these complements as the topic of the sentence introduced by the topic marker <u>ang</u>. We must stress that there can be only one such focused complement in a verbal sentence; all the other four possible complements, if they occur, must be in a non-focus relationship with the verb.

Let us examine each of the five focus constructions for obligatory, optional and absence of complement co-occurrence with the different verb focuses.

(1) Actor focus verbs and their complements

<u>Um-</u> verbs may or may not occur with a goal complement, a locative complement, a benefactive complement and an instrumental complement. The topic will be underlined in the following, and the other complement enclosed in parentheses.

Examples

Tumakbo <u>ang bata</u>.	<u>The child</u> ran.
Kumain (ng saging) <u>ang bata</u>.	<u>The child</u> ate (a banana).
Pumunta (sa palengke) <u>ang nanay</u>.	<u>Mother</u> went (to market).
Bumili <u>ako</u> (ng sapatos) (para sa kaniya).	<u>I</u> bought (a pair of shoes) (for him).
Kumuha <u>siya</u> (ng sabaw) (sa pamamagitan ng sandok).	<u>She</u> got (some soup) (with the ladle).

A benefactive complement only occurs when a goal complement is also present.

<u>Mag-</u> verbs usually have obligatory goal complements. The three other non-focus complements are optional.

Examples

Maglinis <u>ka</u> (ng bahay).	<u>You</u> clean (the house).
Maglinis <u>ka</u> (ng bahay) (sa probinsya).	<u>You</u> clean (the house) (in the province).
Maglinis <u>ka</u> (ng bahay) (para sa kaniya).	<u>You</u> clean (the house) (for her).
Maglinis <u>ka</u> (ng bahay) (sa pamamagitan ng isis).	<u>You</u> clean (the house) (by means of <u>isis</u> leaves).

<u>Mang-</u> verbs like <u>mag-</u> verbs usually have obligatory goal complements. The three other complements are optional.

Examples

Manghuli <u>ka</u> (ng isda).	<u>You</u> catch (fish).
Manghuli <u>ka</u> (ng isda) (sa ilog).	<u>You</u> catch (fish) (in the river).

Manghuli <u>ka</u> (ng isda) (sa
  pamamagitan ng lambat).
<u>You</u> catch (fish) (by
  means of the net).

Manghuli <u>ka</u> (ng isda)
  (para sa pamilya mo).
<u>You</u> catch (fish) (for
  your family).

Certain <u>mang-</u> verbs that do not take an obligatory
goal complement are those that express the goal already
in the verb base: <u>Mangingisda ako (sa dagat)</u>. 'I'll go
fishing (in the sea).'

<u>Ma-</u> verbs do not co-occur with goal complements.
They often occur optionally with locative complements.

<u>Examples</u>

Matulog <u>ka</u> (sa sofa).   <u>You</u> sleep (on the sofa).

Nalunod <u>siya</u> (sa dagat).   <u>He</u> drowned (in the sea).

Nagutom <u>si Ana</u> (sa sine). <u>Ana</u> got hungry (in the
                                 movie house).

(2) Goal focus verbs and their complements

Most verbs in the goal focus construction
(-<u>in</u>/-<u>an</u>/<u>i</u>- verbs) take an actor non-focus complement.
However, there are some that take this complement
optionally.

<u>Examples</u>

Puputulin <u>ang mga puno'</u>. <u>The trees</u> will be cut
                                 down.

Lalaban <u>ang mga damit</u>.   <u>The clothes</u> will be
                                 washed.

The locative complements are almost always
optional. However, some verbs like <u>ilagay</u> 'to put'
require a locative complement.

The most common occurrence of optional benefactive
and instrumental complements is with verbs like the
following.

Bibilhin (ng bata) <u>ang</u>
<u>gamot</u> (sa botika) (para
sa nanay niya).

The <u>medicine</u> will be
bought (by the child)
(from the drugstore)
(for his mother).

Dadalhin (ko) (ng sipit)
<u>ang isda</u> (sa mesa).

(I'll) take <u>the fish</u>
(to the table) (with
chopsticks).

(3) Locative focus verbs and their complements

Some locative focus constructions obligatorily
occur with actor complements.

<u>Examples</u>

Inupuan (niya) <u>ang silya</u>.

(He/she) sat <u>on the
chair</u>.

Sinulatan (ng sekretarya)
<u>ang mga tao</u> (para sa
kandidato).

(The secretary) wrote
<u>to the people</u> (for the
candidate).

Most locative focus verbs, though, take optional
actor complements.

<u>Examples</u>

Dinalhan (niya) (ng
pagkain) <u>ang bata'</u>.

(He) took (some food)
<u>to the child</u>.

Tinataniman (nila) <u>ang</u>
<u>bukid</u>.

<u>The field</u> is being
planted (by them).

Pag-aaralan (ko) <u>ang</u>
<u>kuwento</u>.

<u>The story</u> will be
studied (by me).

With respect to the occurrence of goal complements,
some locative focus verbs have obligatory objects, some
have optional objects, and some have no objects at all.

<u>Examples</u>

With obligatory object

Kinunan (ko) (ng mansanas)
<u>ang basket</u>.

(I) got (some apples)
<u>from the basket</u>.

Pagtatapunan (namin) (ng   (We'll) throw (rubbish)
basura) <u>ang lata</u>.   <u>in the can</u>.

   With optional object

Binalutan (niya) (ng   (He) covered <u>the book</u>
papel) <u>ang libro</u>.   (with paper).

Binayaran (niya) (ng utang)   (He) paid (his debt)
<u>ang babae</u>.   <u>to the woman</u>.

   With no object

Linakaran (niya) <u>ang</u>   (He) walked <u>on the</u>
<u>sahig</u>.   <u>floor</u>.

Tinawanan (niya) <u>ang</u>   (He) laughed <u>at the</u>
<u>babae</u>.   <u>woman</u>.

A benefactive complement can only occur if the
actor complement is also present.

Binalutan (niya) (ng   (He) covered <u>the book</u>
papel) <u>ang libro</u> (para   (with paper) (for the
sa guro').   teacher).

(4) Benefactive focus verbs and their complements

The benefactive focus verbs often take optional
actor complements and either optional or obligatory
goals.

<u>Examples</u>

   With optional actor

Ipinagluto (niya) <u>ako</u>.   Cooking was done <u>for me</u>
                                  (by him/her).

   With optional goal

Itinahi (niya) <u>ako</u> (ng   (He/she) sewed (a
damit).   dress) <u>for me</u>.

With obligatory goal

| Iginawa (niya) <u>ako</u> (ng damit). | (He/she) made (a dress) <u>for me</u>. |
| Dinalhan (niya) <u>ako</u> (ng pagkain). | (He) brought (some food) <u>for me</u>. |

Some verbs that take no goal complements in the benefactive focus may obligatorily require a locative complement.

Examples

| Ikinain (niya) <u>ako</u> (sa pista). | (He) ate <u>for me</u> (at the feast). |
| Itinakbo (niya) <u>ako</u> (sa karera). | (He) ran <u>for me</u> (in the race). |

Some verbs appear with optional locative complements.

Examples

| Ipinagluto (niya) <u>ako</u> (sa kusina'). | (He) cooked <u>for me</u> (in the kitchen). |
| Ipinanghiram (niya) <u>ako</u> (ng pera) (sa bangko). | (He) borrowed (some money) <u>for me</u> (from the bank). |

There are benefactive focus verbs that do not take any instrumental complement, and there are those that take the instrumental complement optionally.

Examples

| Ipinagtanong (niya) <u>ako</u> (nang katulong). | (He) asked (for helpers) <u>for me</u>. |
| Itinahi (niya) <u>ako</u> (ng damit) (sa pamamagitan ng makina). | (She) sewed (a dress) <u>for me</u> (with the sewing machine). |

Benefactive focus verbs therefore may or may not co-occur with any of the non-focus complements.

(5) Instrumental focus verbs and their complements

Verbs that take the instrumental focus generally allow the optional occurrence of actor complements and locative complements.

<u>Examples</u>

Ipinangtulog (niya) (sa kama) <u>ang bata</u>.	(He) used <u>his robe</u> for sleeping (on the bed).
Ipinangalis (niya) (sa Amerika) <u>ang terno</u>.	(She) went (to America) <u>in her terno</u>.

Benefactive complements are optional too.

Ipinanghiram (ko) <u>ang "I.D. card"</u> (ng libro) (para sa bata').	(I) used <u>the I.D. card</u> for borrowing (a book) (for the child).

The instrumental focus verbs therefore may or may not co-occur with any of the non-focus complements.

Generally, therefore, in simple sentences: (1) the topics are obligatory; (2) actor complements are almost always present; (3) instrumental complements are used rarely; (4) transitive verbs with <u>mag-</u> and <u>mang-</u>, except for a few instances, always have goal complements; (5) the locative focus verbs never occur with goal complements; (6) <u>um-</u> verbs are often intransitive and do not require goal complements; but (7) <u>ma-</u> verbs are usually intransitive and so most of the time occur without goal complements.

3. Construction of an Identificational Sentence

Identificational sentences usually reverse the order of Topic and Comment, i.e. the topic precedes the comment instead of following it as is the usual case in predicational sentences. Another characteristic of the identificational sentence is that the marker <u>ang</u> precedes the comment and also the topic if the sentence is definite. In indefinite identificational sentences, the topic is not preceded by the particle <u>ang</u>. Other characteristics of identificational sentences parallel

the predicational sentence. There are verbal and non-
verbal topics and comments for both types, though verbal
topics do not occur in the indefinite variety of the
identificational sentence.

The following chart gives examples of the two
types of sentences with verbal and non-verbal comments.

SUMMARY CHART OF BASIC TAGALOG SENTENCES

SENTENCE TYPE	COMMENT	TOPIC	GLOSS
Predicational			
Verbal Comment	Pumatay	ang sundalo.	The soldier killed (someone).
	Pumatay	ang nagnakaw.	The one who stole (something) killed (someone).
Non-verbal Comment			
Nominal	Doktor	ang Aleman.	The German is a doctor.
Adjectival	Maganda	ang dalaga.	The woman is beautiful.
Prepositional			
Sa phrase	Sa bayan	ang karnabal.	The carnival (will be) in town.
Nasa phrase	Nasa kaniya	ang pera.	The money is with him.
Para sa phrase	Para sa bata	ang laruan.	The toy is for the child.
Existential	May asawa	and babae.	The woman has a spouse.
Adverbial			
Adverb of time	Bukas	ang parada.	The parade is tomorrow.
Adverb of manner	Patihaya	ang bagsak niya.	His fall was flat on his back. (He fell flat on his back.)

SENTENCE TYPE	TOPIC	COMMENT	GLOSS
Identificational			
Definite			
Verbal Comment	Ang nagnakaw	ang pumatay.	The one who stole (something) (was the one who) did the killing.
	Ang sundalo	ang pumatay.	(It was) the soldier (who) did the killing.
Non-verbal Comment			
Nominal	Ang Aleman	ang doktor.	(It is) the German (who is) the doctor.
Adjectival	Ang dalaga	ang maganda.	(It is) the young girl (who is) the beautiful (one).
Prepositional			
Sa phrase	Ang karnabal	ang sa bayan.	(It is) the carnival (which is) in the town.
Nasa phrase	Ang pera	ang nasa kaniya.	(It is) the money (which is) with him (or in his possession).
Para sa phrase	Ang laruan	ang para sa bata.	(It is) the toy (which is) for the child.
Existential	Ang babae	ang may asawa.	(It is) the woman (who) has the spouse.

SENTENCE TYPE	TOPIC	COMMENT	GLOSS
Adverbial	Ang bagsak niya	ang patihaya'.	His fall (was that which was) flat on the back. (He fell flat on his back.)
Indefinite			
Verbal Comment	Sundalo	ang pumatay.	A soldier did the killing.
Non-verbal Comment			
Nominal	Aleman	ang doktor.	A German is the doctor.
Adjectival	Dalaga	ang maganda.	A young girl is the beautiful (one).
Prepositional			
Sa phrase	Karnabal	ang sa bayan.	A carnival (will be) in the town.
Nasa phrase	Pera	ang nasa kaniya.	Money is in his possession.
Para sa phrase	Laruan	ang para sa bata.	A toy is for the child.
Existential	Babae	ang may asawa.	A woman is the one with the spouse.
Adverbial	Bagsak niya	ang patihaya'.	His fall (was) flat on his back. (He fell flat on his back.)

IV. BASIC SENTENCE TYPES

The basic predicational sentence types in Tagalog
are the following.

1. Statement

1.1 Affirmative Statement

Types of Comment   Comment + Topic

Non-verbal

    Nominal   Doktor   ⎡ siya.
                          | si Pedro.
                           ⎣ ang tsuper.

    Adjectival   Maganda   ⎡ ito.
                           | ang baro.
                           ⎣ ka.

    Verbal   Umupo   ⎡ ang guro.
                           | sila.
                           ⎣ si Ginoong Cruz.

Tagalog sentences differ from English sentences
in the following respects.

(1) Tagalog places the comment/topic in the initial
position rather than following the verb as would regu-
larly occur in English sentences.

(2) Tagalog uses non-verbal comments where the
copulative verb to be would be required in English.

A common word order when a comment has more than
one part is for the first part to occur before the
topic and the rest to follow. This is usually true when
the topic is a pronoun.

Comment...Topic...Comment

Guro   siya   sa math.   He teaches math.
Kumanta   kami   sa paaralan.   We sing at school.

Inversion in Sentences

The basic order of the Tagalog predicational statements can be reversed. If the Topic is shifted to
precede the Comment, the inversion marker <u>ay</u> is inserted
between the two elements. Note the re-ordering of the
elements in the sentences in each of the following in-
versions in affirmative statements.

Inversion in Affirmative Statements

<u>Topic</u>   + <u>ay</u>   +   <u>Comment</u>

Topic	ay	Comment
Siya Si Pedro Ang tsuper	ay	doktor.
Ito Ang baro Si Maria Ikaw	ay	maganda.
Ang guro Sila Si Ginoong Cruz	ay	umupo.

Note the use of <u>ikaw</u> for <u>ka</u> in sentence initial
position. <u>Ka</u> never occurs in this position.

Inversion in Statements with Discontinuous Comments

Basic Order

<u>Comment</u>...<u>Topic</u>...<u>Comment</u>

Comment	Topic	Comment
Guro	siya	sa math.
Kumanta	kami	sa paaralan

Inverted Order

<u>Topic</u> + <u>ay</u> + <u>Comment</u>

Topic	ay	Comment
Siya	ay	guro sa math.
Kami	ay	kumanta sa paaralan.

Observe how <u>ay</u> separates or divides the topic from

the comment. This ligature occurs right after the topic of the sentence. This is why ay is sometimes called a comment or predicate marker.

1.2 Negative Statement

Hindi + Comment + Topic

Hindi   Pilipino   si Jorge.

Hindi   maganda   ang babae.

Hindi   umupo   ang guro.

Hindi, a negative particle, is placed before the affirmative sentence to make it negative. When the Topic, however, is a pronoun, that pronoun is shifted before the Comment and thus follows hindi.

Hindi + Pronoun + Comment

Hindi   siya   Pilipino.

Hindi   ito   laruan.

In the inverted order, hindi always follows ay and precedes the Comment.

Topic + ay + hindi + Comment

Si Jorge   ay   hindi   Pilipino.

Ang babae   ay   hindi   maganda.

Ang guro   ay   hindi   umupo.

2. Question

2.1 Yes-no Question

Affirmative Question

Comment + ba + Topic

Amerikano   ba   si Jorge?

Maganda   ba   ito?

Umupo   ba   ang guro?
May pagkain   ba[1]   siya?

Ba is a question marker and usually follows the first full word of a sentence. However, when the topic is the pronoun ka, then ba follows.

Pilipino ka.

Pilipino ka ba?

The yes-no question may be inverted so that the topic is immediately followed by the ba question marker and then by the ay inversion marker.

Topic	+	ba	+	ay	+	Comment
Si Jorge		ba		ay		Amerikano?
Ito		ba		ay		maganda?
Ang guro		ba		ay		umupo?
Siya		ba		ay		may pagkain?
Ikaw		ba		ay		Pilipino?

Note again the switch of forms from ka in the basic order to ikaw in the inverted order.

Negative Question

Hindi	ba	+	Comment	+	Topic
Hindi	ba		Pilipino		si Jorge?
Hindi	ba		umupo		ang guro?
Hindi	ba		guro sa math		si Miss Cruz?

Note the position of ba in the following.

Hindi ba siya Pilipino?

Hindi ka ba Pilipino?

---

[1]Ba follows May pagkain because may cannot occur alone. It is always followed by a noun.

Inversion in Negative Questions

In the following examples, it will be observed that the order of the peripheral elements, e.g. hindi ba, is not changed when the sentence is inverted. The particles are simply appended initially to the Topic + ay + Comment construction.

Hindi	+	ba	+	Topic	+	ay	+	Comment
Hindi		ba		si Jorge		ay		Pilipino?
Hindi		ba		kayo		ay		guro sa math?
Hindi		ba		ang guro		ay		umupo?

Tag Questions

Statement	+	Tag Question
Artista siya,		hindi ba?
Nars si Fe,		hindi ba?
Hindi siya pumunta,		di ba?
Pumunta siya,		di ba?

Hindi ba is a negative tag question in Tagalog. In rapid speech it is reduced to di ba. Unlike in English, there is no affirmative tag question.

Usually negative statements are followed by the tag question ano.

Hindi Amerikano si Art, ano?

Hindi siya pumunta, ano?

Response patterns to yes-no questions

(1) Affirmative response

Oo	+	Comment	+	Topic
Oo,		Amerikano		si Jorge.
Oo,		Pilipino		siya.

Plain oo, 'yes', can stand for the whole affirmative response.

In Tagalog, it is common to agree to a negative comment by saying oo followed by the negative statement.

Q: Hindi Amerikano si Art,   Art isn't American,
    ano?   is he?

R: Oo, hindi siya   Yes, he's not
    Amerikano.   American.

In English, however, one reinforces a negative response by another negative expression, e.g. 'No, he isn't American'.

(2) Negative response

In contrast to a negative sentence, the negative response has two hindi's.

        Hindi, hindi siya Pilipino.

        Hindi, hindi Pilipino si Jorge.

(3) Integration of a negative and an affirmative response

Q: Pilipino ba si Jorge?

R: Hindi, Amerikano siya.

(Hindi... comes from the negative statement, Hindi Pilipino si Jorge and ...Amerikano siya from the affirmative statement, Amerikano si Jorge.)

The comma after hindi stands for a significant pause because what follows is the true information about the topic.

2.2 Questions with Interrogative Words

Interrogative Word   +   Ang Construction

Sino   ang guro mo?

Ano   ang pangalan mo?

```
Alin                    ang lapis mo?

Ilan                    ang babae?
```

Interrogative pronouns often occur initially in sentences followed by _ang_ constructions or their substitutes: Sino ka? Ano ito?

Alin, _saan_, _ano_, and _sino_ are sometimes followed by _sa_ constructions before the _ang_ constructions.

Alin $\begin{bmatrix} \text{sa apat} \\ \text{dito} \end{bmatrix}$ ang anak mo?

Saan $\begin{bmatrix} \text{sa Maynila} \\ \text{dito} \end{bmatrix}$ ang bahay mo?

Question words like _gaano_, _ilan_ and _magkano_ can be followed directly by a noun. When this happens a linker is used between the two.

Interrogative Word + ng + Noun + ang Construction

```
Gaanong bigas           ang kailangan mo?

Magkanong bigas         ang binili mo?

Ilang silya             ang gusto mo?
```

2.3 Inversion of Interrogative Sentences

To invert a question, the _ang_ construction is shifted to initial position in the sentence followed by the question marker _ba_ then the inversion marker _ay_ ending with the interrogative word.

```
        Ang guro mo ba ay sino?
        Ang pangalan mo ba ay ano?
        Ang lapis mo ba ay alin?
        Ang babae ba ay ilan?
        Ang kailangan mo ba ay gaanong bigas?
        Ang binili mo ba ay magkanong bigas?
        Ang gusto mo ba ay ilang silya?
        Ang anak mo ba ay alin sa apat?
```

Where ang constructions are replaced by pronouns, the same order occurs.

> Ikaw ba ay sino?
>
> Ito ba ay ano?

3. Command

3.1 Affirmative Commands

Infinitive forms of the verbs are used for commands and the actor is limited to the second person form of the personal pronoun.

Focus	Verb	Pronoun	Complement
Actor Focus	Maglinis Kumain Manghuli Matulog	ka/kayo	ng bahay. ng almusal. ng daga. ng maaga

			Topic
Goal Focus	Kunin Laban Itapon	mo/ninyo	ang libro. ang damit. ang basura.

If names are used with the commands, they occur first: Maria, maglinis ka ng bahay.

The verbal prefix paki- and the particle nga when occurring in a sentence imply a request. The verb stem with paki- takes an object as the topic of the sentence. The pronoun as actor is limited to the mo/ninyo forms.

Comment (Goal Focus Verb + Actor)		Topic (Goal)
Pakiabot	mo (nga) (nga) ninyo	ang libro.

Note the occurrence of mo before nga and ninyo after nga. Requests of this form are usually said with a rising intonation.

3.2 Negative Commands

Huwag instead of hindi is used in negative commands.

Huwag + um- Verbs (Actor Focus)

Huwag $\begin{bmatrix} kang \\ kayong \end{bmatrix}$ timayo.

Note the use of the linker -ng when the second person ang pronoun actor occurs between huwag and the um- verb.

Huwag + in- Verbs (Goal Focus)

Huwag $\begin{bmatrix} mong \\ ninyong \end{bmatrix}$ inumin ang gatas.

It is important to note the inversion of the position of the pronoun and the verb in the negative command.

Affirmative Command: Inumin mo ang gatas.

Negative Command: Huwag mong inumin ang gatas.

Note the lack of a linker in the affirmative command.

3.3 Inversion in Commands

The inverted form of a command is seldom used. If it is, ikaw is used instead of ka.

Normal Order   Inverted Order

Affirmative Command

Tumalon $\begin{bmatrix} ka. \\ kayo. \end{bmatrix}$ $\begin{bmatrix} Ikaw \\ Kayo \end{bmatrix}$ ay tumalon.

Negative Command

Huwag $\begin{bmatrix} kang \\ kayong \end{bmatrix}$ tumalon. $\begin{bmatrix} Ikaw \\ Kayo \end{bmatrix}$ ay huwag tumalon.

Note that <u>huwag</u> immediately follows <u>ay</u> in the
inverted order.

V. EXPANSION OF SENTENCES

1. General

Basic simple sentences may be expanded or modified
in three ways. First, by attribution in the noun phrase
or in the verbal phrase; second, by compounding, that
is, by the coordination of equivalent syntactic units
or the introduction of a subordinate clause which expresses a cause, consequence, reason, conclusion or the
like in relation to the main clause; and third, by
embedding, that is, the insertion of a whole sentence
after a principal sentence, the inserted sentence
functioning as the Topic of the principal or matrix
sentence. The result of this embedding is a <u>complex</u>
sentence.

2. Expansion by Attribution

2.1 Nominal Expansion

Noun attribution or modification is marked in a
construction by the occurrence of the linker <u>na</u>/-<u>ng</u>
between the modifier and the modified or vice-versa.
The order of quality adjective and noun modified is
usually not fixed, but the linker -<u>ng</u> is always attached
to the first word or element if it ends in a vowel or
-<u>n</u>, be it the modifier or the modified, in the modification structure. <u>Na</u> occurs when the word before it ends
in a consonant.

Adjective + na + Noun (head)	Noun + na + Adjective (head)
lumang kalan 'old stove'	kalang luma' 'stove which is old'
magandang dalaga 'beautiful girl'	dalagang maganda 'girl (who is) beautiful'

```
maputik na sahig              sahig na maputik
 'muddy floor'                 'floor (which is) muddy'

mabait na bata'               batang mabait
 'good child'                  'child (who is) good'

bagong bahay                  bahay na bago
 'new house'                   'house (which is) new'
```

Modifiers before the head noun

A qualifier, say a numeral, can thus be inserted in noun phrases introduced by **ang**, **ng**, or **sa**.

```
ang⎤
ng  | isa-ng bata'            one child
sa  ⎦
```

Adjectives may occur in the same position before the noun.

```
ang⎤
ng  |mabait na bata'          article + 'good child'
sa  ⎦
```

A verb, too, may be used as a modifier to the noun: <u>tumatakbong bata'</u> 'running child'. Note the use of the <u>linker</u> after the verbal modifier.

Possessive pronouns may occur before the noun as modifiers: <u>ang iyong kotse</u> 'your car'.

A demonstrative pronoun may occur as a modifier before the head noun, but it is never preceded by the markers: <u>itong bahay</u> 'this house'.

Quantifiers, that is nouns of measurement, only occur before the head noun as modifier if preceded by a numeral: <u>ang dalawang yardang tela</u> 'the two yards of cloth'.

A head noun may be preceded by two adjective modifiers: <u>ang mahal na matamis na santol</u> 'the expensive, sweet <u>santol</u>'. Note that if the noun has more than one modifier, each one is followed by a linker.

Two or more adjectives may be joined by <u>at</u> 'and';
all modifying the head noun: <u>ang mabait at matalinong</u>
<u>bata</u> 'the good and intelligent child'; <u>ang mabait,</u>
<u>maganda, at mayamang dalaga</u> 'the good, beautiful, and
rich girl'.

Note, however, that when <u>at</u> connects two or more
modifiers, only the last modifier takes the linker.

The order of the pre-head noun modifiers is as
follows:

```
    (1)                    (2)                    (3)
[Noun Marker]         [Possessive            [Numeral-linker
[Demonstrative-   +   Pronoun-linker]   +    (Quantifier)]]
 linker]


    (4)              (5)                      (6)
[Verb-        +   [Adjective (at      +   [Noun-      +   [Noun]
 linker]          adjective)-linker]       linker]        (head)
```

<u>Examples</u>

```
    (1)      (2)       (3)         (5)
   (ang)   (aking)  (tatlong)  (maliliit na)  (anak)
             my       three       small       children


    (1)       (2)          (3)             (5)
  (itong)  (kanilang)  (apat na salop na)  (puting)  (mais)
   these     their      four gantas of      white    corn


    (1)      (2)       (3)          (4)           (5)
   (ang)   (iyong)  (dalawang)  (tumatakbong)  (puting)
             your      two        running        white

     (6)
  (molang)  (kabayo)
   'mola'    horses


    (1)      (2)          (3)                   (4)
   (ang)  (iyong)  (dalawang pirasong)  (nabubulok na)
            your     two pieces of         rotting

     (5)
  (puting)  (keso)
   white    cheese
```

The quantifier (3) never occurs without the numeral
before it: ang (dalawang pirasong) nabubulok na keso,
not *ang (pirasong) nabubulok na keso.

The following example gives a gradual expansion of
the noun phrase by adding pre-head noun modifiers.

ang kabayo

ang molang kabayo

ang puting molang kabayo

ang tumatakbong puting molang kabayo

ang dalawang tumatakbong puting molang kabayo

Modifiers after the headword

It is more natural to have one modifier before the
noun and the rest after it: ang isang batang tumatakbo
'the (one) child who is running'. Note the linker
attached to the head noun if a modifier follows it.

Nouns or noun phrases as modifiers

Nouns or noun phrases may be used as modifiers.
This modification construction is similar to a construction with nouns in apposition, and has the meaning of
the who relative clauses in English.

Si Nenang kapatid ni Rody	Nena, Rody's sister
Si Mang Anton na tsuper ng taksi	Mang Anton, the taxi driver

Unlike the English relative clause, however,
na/-ng in Tagalog does not operate like English 'who'.
The Tagalog particle only connects the modification
structure to the noun it modifies.

A head noun can have more than one phrasal modifier.
The following example has three phrasal modifiers, se-
quenced one after the other.

ang bahay (ni Aling Petra) na (nasa Kalye Herran)
na (katapat ng dating 'Peace Corps Office')

(Aling Petra's) house (which is on Herran Street)
(across from the former Peace Corps Office)

A noun phrase may also have a series of post-noun
modifiers each one modifying the head noun of the
immediately preceding phrase modifier.

ang bahay (ni Aling Maria)ng (asawa ni Mang
Manuel) na (magsasaka)

the house (of Aling Maria) (who is the wife of
Mang Manuel) (who is a farmer)

Verbal constructions as modifiers

Verbs can be used as modification structures after
nouns. Note the following.

Ang batang umiiyak...	The child, crying...
Ang babaing naglalaba...	The woman, washing...
Ang babaing naglalaba sa ilog...	The woman, washing (clothes) by the river...
Ang katulong na naglilinis sa silid...	The helper, cleaning the room...
Ang lalaking sumalok ng tubig kahapon...	The man who fetched water yesterday...

Nasa constructions as modifiers

Modification structures with _nasa_ usually express
the exact location of small, moveable objects.

... librong nasa ibabaw ng piyano...	... book (which is) on the piano...
... taong nasa tabi ng simbahan...	... person (who is) near the church...
... pagong na nasa ilalim ng tulay...	... turtle (which is) under the bridge...
... aklat na nasa ibabaw ng mesa...	... book (which is) on the table...

Naka- constructions as modifiers

Naka- is an adjectival prefix which can be followed
by nouns (limited to things or accessories that can be
worn or put on) and by verb roots, usually um- verbs.

ang babaing	the woman (who is)
nakaluksa'	in mourning
naka-asul	in blue
nakakimona	wearing a native blouse

ang lalaking	the man (who is)
nakatayo'	standing
nakangiti'	smiling

Taga- constructions as modifiers

Taga-, a prefix which was introduced earlier in
these notes as occurring before place nouns, can also
occur before verb roots to mean 'one whose occupation or
work is the one expressed by the verb'.

ang babaing	tagalinis	ng bahay
	tagaluto	ng pagkain
	taga-alaga	ng bata'

the woman	who cleans the house
	who cooks the food
	who takes care of the child

When the question marker ba occurs before these
modification structures, the linker is attached to it:
Ang babae bang naka-uniporme ang guro mo? 'Is the
woman in uniform your teacher?'

An example of a topic with a pre-head and post-head
modification structure is as follows: Ang (bago)ng
bahay (ni Aling Petra)ng (nasa kalye Herŕan) na (katapat
ng dating 'Peace Corps Office').

Note that pre-head modification structures occur
after the ang marker. Note, too, the linker na/-ng
that connects all the modification structures even
within a phrase such as (katapat ng dati)ng '(Peace
Corps Office)'.

2.2 Verbal Expansion

Verbal phrases or comments can be expanded by modification and by complementation.

2.21 Verbal Modification

Except for adverbs indicating time or duration of time, verbal modification is marked by the occurrence of the linker na/-ng between the modifier and the verb or by the adverbial marker nang when the modifier follows the verb.

(1) Modifiers Before the Verb

A limited number of forms with ma- + base are used to modify the verb. They function like adverbs of manner. The verbs occurring after these adjectives are in the infinitive form (i.e., uninflected for aspect).

Ma- Modifier + Linker + Infinitive + Topic
                                    Verb

Madalas   (na)   magsimba   si Lolita.
  'Lolita goes to church frequently.'

Marunong   (na)   magtrabaho   si Pedro.
  'Pedro knows how to work.'

Mahirap   (na)   maglaba.
  'It's hard to wash (clothes).'

The linker na in the examples above is often dropped.

The infinitive verbs in addition to being actor focused as shown by the examples above, can also by the change in verbal affix indicate the other kinds of focuses.

Goal	Madalas linisin ang bahay ni Maria.	The house is cleaned frequently by Maria.
Locative	Madali-ng puntahan ang bahay.	It is easy to get to the house.
Benefactive	Mahirap ibili si Mario ng sapatos.	It is difficult to buy shoes for Mario.

Instrumental   Mahirap ipanghiwa   It is difficult to
               ang kutsilyo ng isda. use the knife for
                                        slicing the fish.

Note that unlike the form of the linker na, the -ng is not dropped.

The ma- verbal modifier occurs before the verb. But when the topic is a pronoun, the pronoun shifts its position before the verb. The linker between the modifier and the verb is then transferred to the pronoun or the particle that immediately precedes the verb.

With an ang phrase topic

Marunong magtrabaho ang katulong ko.   My helper knows how to work.

Maganda-ng manahi si Lolita.   Lolita sews beautifully.

With a pronoun topic

Statement: Marunong siyang magtrabaho.   She knows how to work.

Question: Marunong ba siyang magtrabaho?   Does he know how to work?

Marunong ka bang magluto'?   Do you know how to cook?

Note that when the topic is ka, ba follows it and the linker is transferred to ba.

Pa- with a limited number of bases usually describing position can occur as modifiers before the verb.

Patihaya-ng bumagsak si Pedro.   Pedro landed on his back.

Pabaluktot (na) matutulog si Juan.   Juan will sleep in a curled up position.

Note that unlike the ma- modifiers, the pa- modifiers occur before verbs that can be inflected for aspect.

Verbal forms may modify infinitive verbs which
follow them usually having the same focus. These
verbal modifiers are often in the incompleted aspect
form. Note the following where the topic is first,
then a verbal modifier with the linker, and then the
main verb.

Siyay ⎡umiiyak na umalis.
      ⎣tumatakbong

   She left ⎡crying.
            ⎣running.

Ako'y ⎡nahihiyang ⎡kumain.
      ⎣nahiyang   ⎢humingi ng pera.
                   ⎣magpahinga.

   I'm embarrassed to ⎡eat.
       (ashamed)   ⎢ask for money.
                      ⎣rest.

Ang dayuhan ay ⎡nandidiring ⎡kumain.
               ⎣nandiring   ⎢uminom.
                             ⎣maupo.

   The foreigner ⎡is ⎤ afraid to ⎡eat.
                 ⎣was⎦   ⎢drink.
                                  ⎣sit down.

            ⎡nagpipilit na ⎡pumasok.
Si Maria'y ⎣nagpilit   ⎢manood ng sine.
                           ⎢samahan sa kanto.
                           ⎣ibili' ng sapatos.

                  ⎡going to school.
                  ⎢seeing the movies.
Maria insisted on ⎢having someone go with her
                  ⎢ to the corner.
                  ⎢being bought a pair of
                  ⎣ shoes.

Certain verb-like words are like the English
modals want, like, can, should, must, ought to, etc.
These may be called 'pseudo-verbs'. These pseudo-verbs
are not inflected, and precede an infinitive form. The
following form, or even intervening forms, must be
linked by the ligature na/-ng. Usually, depending upon
the verbal affix of the following infinitive verb, one

of the complements is in focus. The pseudo-verbs however dominate the sentence in the admittance or non-
admittance of actor focus topics. There are three kinds
of modals: those that never take actor focus topics,
like ibig and gusto; those that may or may not take
actor focus topics like kulangan; and those that only
take actor focus topics like maari, puwede, and dapat.

Gusto and ayaw are used without actor focus topics.
Gusto means 'want, like'. Ayaw is the negative form
of gusto. As in a gusto sentence, the verb that follows ayaw is in its infinitive form. Both ayaw and
gusto are often followed by non-focused complements.

Gusto kong lumangoy.	I want to go.
Gusto ng batang maligo.	The child wants to take a bath.
Ayaw ni Pedrong magaral.	Peter doesn't want to study.
Ayaw nina Bert na maglaro'.	Bert and his companions don't want to leave.
Ayaw mo bang magpasyal sa bundok?	Don't you want to take a walk to the mountain?
Ayo-kong kumain ng isda'.	I don't want to eat fish.

Ayoko is a contraction of ayaw + ko.

When followed by in-/i- verbs however, gusto takes
object/goal focus topics.

Gusto niyang isara ang radyo.	He wants a radio.
Gusto ni Rosang basahin ang nobela.	Rosa wants to read the novel.

When gusto is not followed by infinitive verbs, ng
or ang object phrases may follow it. The ng object
complement however is more commonly used. Linkers do
not occur in these sentences.

Gusto ko ng 'coke'.	I want a coke.
Ayaw ng bata (ang 'coke').	The child doesn't want a coke.

Alam and Ibig

Other pseudo-verbs that function like gusto are alam, 'know', and ibig, 'want'.

Examples

    Alam kong magalaga ng manok.

    Alam mo bang magalaga ng manok?

    Alam niyang maglaba.

    Alam ba niyang maglaba?

    Ibig kong mag-'shopping'.

    Ibig mo bang mag-'shopping'.

    Ibig (na) magsine ni Jaime.

    Ibig bang magsine ni Jaime.

    Ibig ba ni Jaimeng magsine?

Note again the use of linkers right before the infinitive form of the verb. Na before the infinitive form of the verb is often dropped.

Kailangan is used with or without actor focus topics. Kailangan can occur with a focused or non-focused actor complement when the infinitive verb that follows is actor focus.

    Kailangan akong magpasyal.   I must take a walk.

Again, the non-focused actor complement is more often used than the focused one.

Maari, dapat, and puwede only take actor focus topics when the infinitive verb that follows them is actor focus.

Examples

    Maari akong magturo sa Pilipinas.

Puwede ba akong magturo sa Pilipinas?

Dapat ka bang magturo sa Pilipinas?

Except for <u>gusto</u>, <u>ibig</u> and <u>alam</u> which cannot focus on the actor complement, all the other modal sentences can focus on any topic depending upon the verbal affix of the infinitive verb.

Further examples of the three types of modals follow. If you do not understand the sentences, practice using the dictionary or the glossary for the lessons.

<u>Gusto</u>:

Usual:	Gusto kong bumili ng manok.
Goal Focus:	Gusto kong bilhin ang manok.
Locative Focus:	Gusto kong bilhan ang tindahan ng sigarilyo.
Benefactive Focus:	Gusto kong ibili ang nanay ng sapatos.
Instrumental Focus:	Gusto kong ipangbili ng sapatos ang pera ng tatay.

<u>Kailangan</u>:

Actor Focus:	Kailangan akong uminom ng gamot.
Goal Focus:	Kailangan kong inumin ang gamot.
Locative Focus:	Kailangan kong inuman ang baso ko.
Benefactive Focus:	Kailangan kong iinum siya sa handaan.
Instrumental Focus:	Kailangan kong ipanginom ang tasa.

<u>Maari</u>:

Actor Focus: Maari akong magluto ng pag-
                      kain.

Goal Focus: Maari kong lutiin ang pagkain.

Locative Focus: Maari kong lutuan ang bagong
                      kawali.

Benefactive Focus: Maari kong ipagluto siya ng
                      pagkain.

Instrumental Focus: Maari kong ipangluto ang
                      kuryente.

(2) <u>Modifiers after the verb</u>

<u>Ma</u>- modifiers may occur after the verb though some <u>ma</u>- modifiers can only occur before the verb.

One can say: Marunong magtrabaho ang kalutong ko. 'My helper knows how to work well.'

But one cannot say: Magtrabaho-nang marunong ang katulong ko.

Most <u>ma</u>- modifiers however can occur before and after the verb.

Madalas (na) maglaba ang nanay.

Naglalaba nang madalas ang nanay.

When the modifiers occur after the verb, they are preceded by the adverbial marker <u>nang</u> and the verbs they follow are not in the infinitive form but are inflected for aspect.

<u>Examples</u>

Completed	Tumakbo siya nang marahan.	He ran slowly.
Incompleted	Tumatakbo si Maria nang madalas.	She runs frequently.
Contemplated	Tatakbo ang bata nang mabilis.	The child will run fast.

Although pa- modifiers may occur before the verb they are also often found in post-verbal position, describing the manner or position of the action indicated by the verb stem.

Bumagsak siya nang patihaya'.	He landed on his back.
Lumakad siya nang paluhod.	She walked on her knees.
Natulog ang bata nang pabaluktot.	The child slept in a curled up position.

The verbs can be inflected for aspect.

$$\left.\begin{matrix}\text{Umupo}\\\text{Umuupo}\\\text{Uupo}\end{matrix}\right\} \text{siya nang patingkayad.}$$

$$\text{He}\begin{bmatrix}\text{sat}\\\text{is sitting}\\\text{will sit}\\\text{(squat)}\end{bmatrix}\text{on his heels.}$$

Naka- constructions are preceded by the linker when they occur after the topic, and by nang when preceded by the verb. The verb can be in any aspect.

$$\left.\begin{matrix}\text{Natutulog}\\\text{Natulog}\end{matrix}\right\}\text{siyang}\begin{bmatrix}\text{nakabaluktot.}\\\text{nakaupo'.}\\\text{nakadapa'.}\\\text{nakabuka ang bibig.}\end{bmatrix}$$

$$\text{He}\begin{bmatrix}\text{is sleeping}\\\text{slept}\end{bmatrix}\begin{bmatrix}\text{in a curled up position.}\\\text{sitting down.}\\\text{on his stomach.}\\\text{with his mouth wide open.}\end{bmatrix}$$

$$\text{Siyáy}\begin{bmatrix}\text{natutulog}\\\text{natulog}\end{bmatrix}\text{nang nakadapa.}$$

Verbal modifiers can be intensified by the process of reduplication or by the addition of adverbial intensifiers to the verb base.

Intensifiers

(+ ubod)	Tumakbo siya nang ubod ng bilis.	He ran very fast.
(+ napaka-)	Tumawa siya nang napakalakas.	He laughed very loudly.
(+ pagka- and redup. of base)	Umiyak siya nang pagkalakas-lakas.	She cried very loudly.
(+ redup. of base)	Lumakad siya nang dahan-dahan.	He walked very slowly.

Adverbs of time usually occur after the verbs. They can occur after the topic too. But they always follow the pronoun-topic.

Completed	Kumain kanina/kahapon si Pedro.	Pedro ate a while ago/yesterday.
Contemplated	Kakain bukas/mamaya ang bisita.	The visitor will eat tomorrow/a little later.
Incompleted	Kumakain ngayon ang bata'.	The child is eating now.
Completed	Kumain si Pedro kanina/kahapon.	
Contemplated	Kakain ang bisita bukas/mamaya.	
Incompleted	Kumakain ang bata ngayon.	
Completed	Kumain ka kahapon.	
Contemplated	Kakain ako bukas.	
Incompleted	Kumakain siya ngayon.	

Note that certain time expressions only occur with certain aspects of the verbs.

Time expressions can precede the verbs. But when they do, the inversion marker ay follows them or a significant pause follows before the verb is said.

Kanina ay tumawag si Maria   Maria called him a
sa kaniya.   while ago.

Kanina, tumawag si Maria
sa kaniya.

     Adverbial particles na and pa when added after
verbs indicate completion or non-completion of the
action. Generally, na indicates completed or terminated
action.

Kumain ka ⎡na ba?
        ⎣na ba ⎡siya?
              ⎢si Maria?
              ⎣ang bisita?

                       Have you   ⎤
                       Has ⎡she   ⎢eaten already?
                              ⎢Maria   ⎢
                              ⎣the visitor⎦

Oo, kumain ka ⎡na.   Yes, you have, etc.
          ⎣na ⎡siya.
              ⎢si Maria.
              ⎣ang bisita.

Note how na precedes all the topics except ka. This is
true for other monosyllabic pronouns too.

     Most Tagalog speakers of English equate 'already'
with na, but the latter has a wider distribution than
English 'already'.

     Pa-, 'still, yet', in contrast to na, signals
incompleted action. Note how the incompleteness of the
action is also signaled by the incompleted aspect of
the verb that precedes it.

Kumakain pa ako.   I'm still eating.

Kumakain pa ba siya?   Is she still eating?

Kumakain ka pa ba?   Are you still eating?

     Note how pa occurs immediately after the verb un-
less ka (or any monosyllabic pronoun) is present. Note
too that when ba is present it follows pa.

2.22 Verbal Complementation

Verbal comments can be expanded to include as many as four complements. Each complement may have its own modifier. It is not common to come across a normal Tagalog sentence where all these complements are present. At the most two or three complements may be used in sentences.

Examples of expansion of a basic sentence by means of complementation follow.

Basic Sentence: Nagluto ang nanay. Mother cooked.

+ Goal Complement

| Nagluto ang nanay ng adobo. | Mother cooked adobo. |

+ Locative Complement

| Nagluto ang nanay ng adobo sa kapitbahay. | Mother cooked adobo at the neighbors. |

+ Benefactive Complement

| Nagluto ang nanay ng adobo sa kapitbahay para sa amin. | Mother cooked adobo at the neighbors for us. |

+ Instrumental Complement

| Nagluto ang nanay ng adobo sa kapitbahay para sa amin (sa pamamagitan) ng baboy na dala ng tatay. | Mother cooked adobo at the neighbors for us by means of the pork Father brought with him. |

Examples of the five verbal complements with their possible substitutes are as follows, with the verb followed by the topic then the object, locative, benefactive and instrumental complements.

Actor Focus

| Bumili ang bata ng tinapay sa tindahan para sa kapatid niya (sa pamama-gitan) ng pera niya. | The child bought bread from the store for his brother/sister (by means of) his money. |

Bumili ito nito doon para dito (sa pamamagitan) nito.	This (one) bought this from there for here (by means of) this.
Bumili siya nito sa kanila para sa kaniya.	He bought this from them for her.
Bumili si Pedro nito kay Aling Nena para kay Mrs. Cruz.	Pedro bought this from Aling Nena for Mrs. Cruz.

Goal Focus

Binili ang tinapay ng bata.	A child bought the bread.
Binili ito nito.	This (one) bought this.
Binili niya.	He bought it.

3. Expansion by Compounding

Two or more syntactically equivalent units can be joined in a coordinate structure by the use of conjunctions: at 'and', ni...ni 'neither...nor', pero/subalit/ngunit/datapwat 'but', o 'or'. These conjunctions may occur between words, phrases, or sentences.

Words

ikaw		ako	you and I
itim	at	puti	black and white
aso		pusa'	dog and cat
tumakbo		tumalon	ran and jumped

maganda, mabait, at mayaman	beautiful, good, and rich
ikaw o ako	you or I
ni ikaw ni ako	neither you nor I
maganda pero salbake	beautiful but bad

Phrases

ang bata at ang matanda'	the young and the old
ang buhay mo o ang salapi mo	your life or your money

ni kapatid mo ni magulang mo	neither your brothers nor your parents
ang yaman nga pero ang tanda naman	rich but old

Sentences

Basic sentences may be expanded into <u>compound</u> sentences when joined by two types of conjunctions. One type, the <u>coordinator</u>, joins two sentences of equal rank and only occurs between the two sentences joined together.

The Tagalog coordinators resemble the English coordinators in function. They are the same as the conjunctions used to join words and phrases illustrated above.

Coordinators

Tumugtog si Maria ng piyano at kumanta si Pedro.	Maria played the piano and Peter sang.
Siguro, tutugtog si Mario ng piyano o sasayaw si Maria.	Maybe Mario will play the piano or Maria will dance.
Maganda ang babae pero/ subalit/ngunit/datapwat pangit ang lalake.	The woman is beautiful but the man is ugly.

Subordinating conjunctions join two sentences, one of which is dependent or subordinate to the other. The subordinate sentence follows the subordinating conjunction and modifies the principal or independent sentence. The subordinators are as follows.

dahil/kasi/sapagkat	because, because of
kaya	therefore, so, hence
kahit (na)/bagaman (at)	although, even if, even though
(mag)mula (nang)	since, ever since
samantala/habang	while, during

upang/at nang	in order to, so that
at baka	lest, for
nang	when
kung, (ka) pag	if

Examples follow.

Umalis din siya bagaman/ kahit na bumabagyo.	He left although there was a storm.
Hindi na kami nakapag- trabaho (mag)mula nang dumating siya.	We haven't been able to work ever since he came.
Magpahinga ka naman habang/samantala-ng natutulog siya.	(You) rest while he's sleeping.
Tumangan ka ng mahigpit upang/*at nang hindi ka mabulog.	Hold tight so that you won't fall.
Huwag kang magbasa' *at baka ikaw ay sipunin/ (ka).	Don't get wet lest you catch a cold.
Hindi siya nakaalis dahil/kasi/sapagkat wala siyang pera.	He wasn't able to leave because he had no money.
Pinalo siya ng tatay kaya lumayas si Mario.	His father whipped him so Mario ran away.
Nagalit muna ang maestra bago siya('y) su magot.	The teacher became angry before he answered (her).
Patay na ang ilaw sa bahay nang dumating siya.	The lights were (already) out when he came.
Isusi mo ang pinto kung/kapag aalis ka na.	Lock the door if you're about to leave.

Sentences joined by subordinators (except those marked with *) unlike those joined by coordinators can be inverted with the conjunction and the sentence it introduces placed before the first sentence.

Example: Kahit na bumabagyo, umalis din siya.

4. Expansion by Embedding

A complex sentence may be formed by embedding or inserting a sentence in a principal or matrix sentence, the embedded or inserted sentence functioning as the topic of the matrix sentence. For example: (Sinabi ng bata) na (umuwi na ang maestra). 'The child said that the teacher had already gone home.'

Na in the sentence above connects a whole sentence, umuwi na ang maestra, 'the teacher had already gone home', to the matrix sentence, sinabi ng bata, 'the child said'. The embedded sentence acts as a goal or direct object in the whole sentence. This differentiates this construction from a subordinate sentence where one of the clauses only modifies the matrix sentence.

Verb (Goal Focus)	Actor	Linker	Object/Goal	
Sinabi	ng bata	na	umuwi na	ang maestra.
			Pred	Topic
Matrix sentence		linker	Embedded Goal	

Other examples of this type of sentence are the following.

Totoo na/-ng magugunao ang mundo.	It's true that the world will disintegrate.
Tama naman na/-ng magalit ka sa kanya.	It's (really) right that you be mad at him.
May katwiran na/-ng mayamut ka.	It's understandable that you (should) get irritated.
Umaasa ako na darating ka.	I'm hoping that you will come.

VI. COMPARATIVE CONSTRUCTIONS

Persons, things, and actions may be compared in
terms of degrees of equality, superiority, or inferiority. These degrees of comparison are indicated in
Tagalog sentences by comparative markers mas, sa/kaysa
(sa), (kay sa) kay/kina to signal the comparative
degree of inferiority or superiority; magkasing/kasing
to signal the degree of equality; and the affix pinaka-
to express the superlative degree.

1. Degree of Equality

To express the same degree of equality in nouns
or verbs being compared, the adjectival root is preceded
by the following.

Magkasing 'equally'

Comparative Marker	Adjective	Verb (Infinitive)	Topic
	puti		sila.
Magkasing	taas	tumakbo	ang babae at ang lalake.
	bilis		si Nena at si Lily.

Kasing 'as...as'

Comparative Marker	Adjec- tive	Verb	Ng Phrase	Topic
	dunong		ni Nena	si Lily.
Kasing	ikli	tumakbo	ng baro mo	ang baro ko.
	bagal		noon	ito.

Note that in the sentences where kasing is the
comparative marker, the two noun phrases have different
markers. One is a ng phrase which functions as the
'standard'; the other, which is a noun being compared
to the standard, is an ang phrase (the topic of the
sentence).

When inverted, observe what happens to the ng phrase.

Topic	ay	Comment
Si Lily	ay	kasing dunong ni Nena.
Ang baro ko	ay	kasing ikli ng baro mo.
Ito	ay	kasing bagal timakbo noon.

The ng phrase goes with the Comment introduced by the comparative marker rather than with the Topic.

2. Comparative Degree

When the quality in one noun being compared is more than the quality in the other, the phrase markers kaysa (sa) or sa before common nouns or kaysa kay or kina before personal proper nouns occur before the noun being compared.

The comparative form of adjectives is marked by mas, lalo, or higit na before the adjectival non-verbal predicates.

Mas malakas si Jaime kaysa kay/kay Juan.

Lalong matibay ang Volkswagen kaysa sa/kaysa/sa Fiat.

Higit na mabagal tumakbo ang kalesa kaysa sa/ kaysa/sa karetela.

Kaysa kay is the counterpart of kaysa sa when occurring before personal proper nouns. Both kaysa sa and kaysa kay may be reduced to kaysa, sa, or kay respectively.

The sentences above may have been the result of the combination of two simple sentences being compared:

Malakas si Juan.
(Pero) mas malakas si Jaime.

Matibay ang Fiat.
(Pero) lalong matibay ang Volkswagen.

Mabagal tumakbo ang kalesa.
(Pero) higit na mabagal tumakbo ang karetela.

3. Superlative Degree

The superlative degree of the adjective is expressed by the affix pinaka- prefixed to the ma-
adjectives or to the adjectival roots that do not need
the ma- affix.

maganda	→	pinakamaganda
popular	→	pinakapopular
mura	→	pinakamura
mainit	→	pinakamainit

The superlative degree of adjectives usually occurs
before the noun they modify.

Pinakamagandang artista siya.

Sino ang pinakamagandang artista?

Pinakamagaling na guro si Lydia.

Note the presence of the linker between the adjective
and the noun modified. The linker disappears when what
follows immediately is the topic: Pinakamaganda siya/
ang guro ko.

VII. CAUSATIVE SENTENCES

In the indicative (simple) or non-causative sentences the actor is the doer of the action. However
there is another set of sentences called causative
sentences where the actor "causes" an action to be
done. This act of causation is indicated by the verbal
affix pa-.

There are two types of causative sentences: the
single causative sentences and the double causative
sentences. The single causative sentence is marked by
a single pa- affix while the double causative sentence
is marked by papa-.

1. Single Causative Sentences

The causative actor focus affix is <u>mag-</u> combined with <u>pa-</u> (magpa-). There are three ways by which the single act of causation is consummated.

(1) The causative actor may cause a non-causative actor to do the action.

Focus	(1) Verb	(2) Causative Actor	(3) Object	(4) Non-causative Actor
Actor Focus:	Nagpaluto	ako	ng pansit	sa kusinera.
	'had cook'	'I'	'noodles'	'the cook'

'I caused the cook to prepare some noodles.'

The actor who is caused by the causative actor in the sentence to perform the action is the non-causative actor complement and is introduced by the non-focus marker <u>sa/kay</u> or an appropriate substitute.

Other verbs that belong to this class are: <u>magpakulot</u> 'to have a permanent', <u>magpagupit</u> 'to have a hair cut', <u>magpalaba</u> 'to have clothes laundered', <u>magpalinis</u> 'to have something cleaned', <u>magpatahi</u> 'to have clothes sewn', <u>magpakuha</u> 'to cause someone to get something', <u>magpabili</u> 'to cause someone to buy something', <u>magpahula</u> 'to cause someone to tell one's fortune'.

The non-causative actor is sometimes implied in the verb and is therefore optional.

Verb	Actor	Object	Non-causative Actor
Nagpagupit 'caused to be cut'	ako 'I'	(ng buhok) 'hair'	(sa barbero). 'by the barber'
Nagpakulot 'caused to be curled'	ako 'I'	(ng buhok) 'hair'	(sa mangungulot). 'by the beauti- cian'

Sometimes even the goal, when understood from the verb, is dropped: <u>Nagpagupit ako</u>. 'I caused him to cut (my hair).'

(2) The causative actor without causing another actor to perform the action may <u>directly</u> cause the object to undergo the action: Nagpatulog ako ng bata. 'I caused the child to sleep.'

Other verbs that belong to this class are <u>magpakain</u> 'to cause someone to eat, to feed someone', <u>magpaligo</u> 'to bathe or cause someone to bathe', <u>magpasuso</u> 'to breastfeed/bottlefeed a baby', <u>magpaaral</u> 'to cause (someone) to study/to send (someone) to school'.

(3) The causative actor may cause himself to undergo the action named by the base: Nagpaganda siya. 'She caused herself to become beautiful/She beautified herself.'

Other verbs that belong to this class are <u>magpataba</u> 'to cause (oneself) to become stout', <u>magpapayat</u> 'to cause (oneself) to slim down', <u>magpagaling</u> 'to cause (oneself) to become well'.

The verbal affix markers of the causative verb indicating that the goal complement is in focus are <u>ipa-</u> and <u>pa--an</u>. The first is more common.

Examples

súlat	write	ipa-súlat	to cause something to be written
tahí'	sew	ipa-tahí'	to cause something to be sewn
línis	clean	ipa-línis	to cause something to be cleaned

If the non-causative goal focus affix is <u>-an</u>, the causative goal focus affix is <u>pa--an</u>.

Examples

| labá | to wash clothes | palabán ⎤ palabhán⎦ | to cause something to be washed |

bukás	to open	pabuksán	to cause some-

bukás   to open   pabuksán   to cause some-
            (also, ipabukás)   thing to be
                               opened

If the actor is in focus which does not do the causing, the focus affixes are pa--in and papag--in. The affix is usually pa--in, but when the indicative/ non-causative source is a mag- verb, papag--in is used instead.

Examples

pa--in with um- verbs

| sumúlat | to write | pasulátin | to cause some- one to write something |
| manahí | to sew | patahiín | to cause some- one to sew something |

papag--in with mag- verbs

| maglínis | to clean | papagli- nísin | to cause some- one to clean something |
| maglabá | to wash clothes | papagla- bahín | to cause some- one to wash clothes |

Pa- of papag- is often dropped in rapid speech: paglinisin 'to cause to clean', paglabahín 'to cause to wash clothes'.

The causative locative focus affix is pa--an, the causative instrumental focus affix is ipapang- usually shortened to ipang-, and the causative benefactive focus affix is similar to the causative goal focus affix (ipa- or ipagpa-). Again ipagpa- seems to correspond to mag- verbs.

In summary, here is a causative sentence showing each of the five complements in focus and the different aspectual forms of the verbs. The following gives the possible forms with bumili 'to buy'. Numbers in the chart correspond to numbers given in the gloss. In each case, the grammatical topic is underlined.

(1) *Focus Verb (Aspect)*	(2) Causative Actor	(3) Non-Causative Actor	(4) Goal	(5) Locative	(6) Benefactive	(7) Instrumental
CAF						
Magpabili (N)						
Nagpabili (Cmp.)	ka	sa katulong	ng tinapay	sa tindahan	para sa bata	sa pamamagitan ng pera ng napulot ko.
Nagpapabili (Inc.)						
Magpapabili (Con.)						
NCAF						
Pabilin (N)						
Pinabili (Cmp.)	mo	ang katulong	(4)	(5)	(6)	(7)
Pinabibili (Inc.)						
Pabibilin (Con.)						

*Aspect: (Asp.), Neutral (N), Completed (Cmp.), Incompleted (Inc.), Contemplated (Con.).

Focus: CAF (Causative Actor Focus), NCAF (Non-causative Actor Focus), CGF (Causative Goal Focus), CLF (Causative Locative Focus), CBF (Causative Benefactive Focus), CIF (Causative Instrumental Focus).

	(2)	(3)	(4)	(5)	(6)	(7)
CGF Ipabilí (N) Ipinabilí (Cmp.) Ipinabibilí (Inc.) Ipabibilí (Con.)	(2)	sa katulong	ang tina-<u>pay</u>	(5)	(6)	(7)
CLF Pabilhán (N) Pinabilhán (Cmp.) Pinabibilhán (Inc.) Pabibilhán (Con.)	(2)	(3)	ng tinapay	ang tinda-<u>han</u>	(6)	(7)
CBF Ipabilí (N) Ipinabilí (Cmp.) Ipinabibilí (Inc.) Ipabibilí (Con.)	(2)	(3)	(4)	sa tindahan	<u>ang</u> <u>bata</u>	(7)

CIF				
Ipapangbilí (N)	(2)	(3)	(4)	(5)
Ipinapangbilí (Cmp.)				para sa bata
Ipinapangbibilí (Inc.)				ang perang napulot ko
Ipapangbibilí (Con.)				

Gloss: You (cause) have the helper buy bread for the child from the store
       2   1   3   1 4   6   5

      by means of the money I found.
            7

There seems to be a preferred word order or sequence for the <u>actor</u> and the <u>topic</u> in causative
sentences. Both seek either second or third position
in the sentence. The other positions, however, as shown
in the chart, are also possible. Pronouns on the other
hand always seek no later than the third position in
the sentence. For example, it is wrong to say: *Ipabili mo sa katulong ng tinapay sa tindahan [ako]. 'Have
(you) the helper buy me bread from the store.' The
more natural order is to shift the pronoun to the third
position in the sentence: Ipabili mo ako...

A comparison of the non-causative and causative
verbal forms is shown in the following chart.

Focus	Non-Causative		Causative	
Actor focus	-um-	tumahí'/ manahí'	magpa-	Magpatahí'
Goal focus	-in	tahiín	ipa-	Ipatahí'
Non-causative actor focus			pa--in	Patahiín
Locative focus	pag--an	pagtahián	pagpa--an	Pagpatahián
Benefactive focus	i-	itahí'	i(pag)pa-	Ipagpatahí'
Instrumental focus	ipang-	ipangtahí'	ipapang-	Ipapangtahí'
Actor focus	-um-	sumulat	magpa-	Magpasúlat
Goal focus	i-	isulat	ipa-	Ipasúlat
	-in	sulatin		
Non-causative actor focus			pa--in	Pasulátin
Locative focus	-an	sulatan	pa--an	Pasulátan
Benefactive focus	i-	isulat	ipapag-	Ipapagsúlat/ isúlat
Instrumental focus	ipang-	ipangsulat	ipapang-	Ipapangsúlat

Actor focus	mag-	maglabá	magpa-	Magpalabá
Goal focus	-an	labán	pa--an	Palabán
Non-causative actor focus			papag--in	Papaglabahín
Locative focus	pag--an	paglabhán	papag--an	Papaglabhán
Benefactive focus	ipag-	ipaglabá	ipapag-	Ipapaglabá
Instrumental focus	ipang-	ipanglabá	ipapang-	Ipapanglabá
Actor focus	mag-	maglínis	magpa-	Magpalínis
Goal focus	-in	linísin	ipa-	Ipalínis
Non-causative actor focus			pa--in	Palinisín
Locative focus	-an	linísan	pa--an	Palinisán
Benefactive focus	ipag-	ipaglínis	ipapag-	Ipapaglínis
Instrumental	ipang-	ipanglínis	ipapang-	Ipapanglínis

The aspect formations may be illustrated as follows, using _gupit_ 'to cut' as a sample.

Magpa- Verb: (Causative Actor Focus)

The _magpa-_ verb is inflected like the _mag-/ma-_ verbs to indicate not begun (m-) or begun (n-) action. But unlike the _maka-_ affix, only the last CV of the _magpa-_ affix is reduplicated to indicate non-completed action.

Neutral   [_magpa-_ + root]   magpagupít   to have a hair-
                                                cut

Completed [_nagpa-_ + root]   nagpagupít   had a haircut

Incom-   [_nagpapa-_ + root] nagpapagupít having a hair-
pleted   cut

Contem-   [_magpapa-_ + root] magpapagupít will be having
plated   a haircut

Pa--an Verb: (Causative Goal Focus)

Neutral	[pa- + root + -an]	pagupitán
Completed	[pina- + root + -an]	pinagupitán
Incompleted	[pina- + redup root + -an]	pinagugupitán
Contemplated	[pa- + redup root + -an]	pagugupitán

Pa--in Verb: (Non-Causative Actor Focus)
(Source: um- verb)

Neutral	[pa- + root + -in]	pagupitín
Completed	[pina- + root]	pinagupít
Incompleted	[pina- + redup root]	pinagugupít
	[pinapa- + root]	pinapagupít
Contemplated	[pa- + redup root + -in]	pagugupitín
	[papa- + root + -in]	papagupitín

When the verb stem is a mag- verb, papag--in
replaces the pa--in verbal affix.

Papag--in Verb: (Non-Causative Actor Focus)
(Source: mag- verb)

Base: luto   'to cook'

Neutral	[papag- + root + -in]	papaglutúin
Completed	[pinapag- + root]	pinapaglúto'
Incompleted	[pinapag- + redup root]	pinapaglulúto'
	[pinapapag- + root]	pinapapaglúto'
Contemplated	[papag- + redup root + -in]	papaglulutúin
	[papapag- + root + -in]	papapaglutúin

The pa- of papag- is often dropped in rapid
speech.

Note that the non-actor causative types of focus
either get the first syllable of the affix or the root
reduplicated. The difference in their use is a matter
of style. The accepted form which is found in the
Balarila, the official grammar book of the Institute of
National Language, is the partially reduplicated root

word. But in spoken, conversational language, the reduplicated affix is more common.

2. Double Causative Sentences

Some verb roots take a double causative action with the addition of another pa-. In these sentences, the primary causative actor causes a secondary causative actor to cause the object or the non-causative actor to perform the action.

These double causative verbs are commonly found in identificational sentences.

Example

Primary Causative Actor	Ang + Magpapa- Verb	Secondary Causative Actor	Object
Ako	ang nagpapatulog	sa katulong	sa anak ko niya.

'I was the one who asked/caused the maid to make his child go to bed.'

When the secondary causative actor is focused the papagpa- affix replaces magpapa-.

Secondary Causative Actor	Ang + Siyang + Papagpa- Verbs	Primary Causative Actor	Object
Ang katulong ko	ang siyang pinapag-patulog	ko	sa anak niya.

'My helper/maid was the one I asked to have the child go to bed.'

In rapid speech, pag- of papagpa- is dropped.

When the object/non-causative actor is in focus, the papa- verbal affix is prefixed to the verb root.

Example

Object	Ang + Papa- Verbs	Primary Causative Actor	Secondary Causative Actor
Ang anak niya	ang pinapatulog	ko sa	katulong ko.

'His child was the one I asked my maid to put to sleep.'

The following examples illustrate the non-causative, the single causative, and the double causative sentences.

(Source: um- verb [transitive])

Non-causative Action

[-um-]

AF   Ang anak niya ang kumain ng lugaw.   His child was the one who ate the porridge.

[-in]

GF   Ang lugaw ang kinain ng anak niya.   It was the porridge which was eaten by his child.

Single Causative Action

[magpa-]

CAF   Ang alila ang nagpakain ng lugaw sa anak niya.   The maid was the one who fed his child porridge.

[pa--in]

CDF   Ang anak niya ang pinakain ng lugaw ng alila.   His child was the one fed porridge by the maid.

[ipa-]

CGF   Ang lugaw ang ipinakain   It was the porridge
       sa anak niya ng alila.   which was fed to his
                                       child by the maid.

Double Causative Action

[magpapa-]

PCAF   Ako ang nagpapakain sa   I was the one who asked
       alila ng lugaw sa anak   the maid to feed
       niya.   porridge to his child.

[papagpa--in]

SCAF   Ang alila ang pinapag-   The maid was the one I
       pakain ko ng lugaw sa   asked to feed porridge
       anak niya.   to his child.

[ipapa-]

DCGF   Ang lugaw ang ipinapa-   It was the porridge
       kain ko sa alila sa   which I asked the
       anak niya.   maid to feed to his
                                         child.

[papa--in]

DCDF   Ang anak niya ang   His child was the one
       pinapakain ko ng lugaw   I asked the maid to
       sa alila.   feed porridge to.

(Source: <u>ma</u>- verb [intransitive])

Non-causative Action

[ma-]

AF   Ang anak niya ang   His child was the one
       natulog.   who slept.

Single Causative Action

[magpa-]

CAF   Ang alila ang nagpa-   The maid was the one
       tulog sa anak niya.   who put his child to
                                       sleep.

[pa--in]

| CDF | Ang anak niya ang pinatulog ng alila. | His child was the one put to sleep by the maid. |

Double Causative Action

[magpapa-]

| PCAF | Ako ang nagpapatulog ng anak niya sa alila. | I was the one who asked the maid to put his child to sleep. |

[papagpa--in]

| SCAF | Ang alila ang pinapag-patulog ko sa anak niya. | The maid was the one I asked to put his child to sleep. |

[papa--in]

| DCGF | Ang anak niya ang pinapatulog ko sa alila. | His child was the one I asked the maid to put to sleep. |

VIII.   TOPICLESS SENTENCES IN TAGALOG

A special set of sentences in Tagalog may be viewed as topicless, that is, ang phrases do not occur in this set of sentences. There are five types of topicless sentences.

1.   Existential Sentence

An existential sentence consists of the particles may or wala denoting the existence or nonexistence of the following noun.

May tao sa bahay.	There's someone in the house.
Walang mais sa palengke.	There's no corn in the market.
Mayroong klase bukas.	There's class tomorrow.

Walang tao.   There's no one.

Notice that the existential phrase may occur with or without complements. The existential constructions may/mayroon and wala are topicless when followed by actor focus verbs.

May nagnakaw ng pera ko.	Somebody stole my money.
Walang sumaklolo sa nalunod.	No one helped the one who drowned.
Mayroong tumatakbo sa kuwarto.	There is someone running in the room.

Note the use of linkers after wala and mayroon.

With goal focused verbs following the existential particles, actor-topics appear in the existential sentences.

May gagawin ako.	I'll do something.
May hinahanap siya.	He's looking for something.
May kinuha ang bata.	The child took something.
Walang lulutuin ang nanay.	Mother doesn't have anything to cook.
Mayroong kakanin ang aso.	The dog has something to eat.

When inverted, the existential phrases are clearly the goal-comments of the sentences.

May gagawin ako. → Ako ay may gagawin.
                                 I have something to do.

When the goal-comment is expanded, the goal of the goal focused verb is connected to it by the linker na/-ng.

Mayhahanaping bata siya. → Siya ay may
hahanaping bata.

He's going to look for
a child.

2. Phenomenal Sentence

Phenomenal sentences may consist of a closed class
of verbs or adjectives stating certain acts of nature
or natural phenomena. The verb may occur without any
complement. Usually adverbial or locative complements
follow these phenomenal adjectives or verbs. The -um-
affix is added on to nouns of natural phenomena like
áraw 'sun', ulán 'rain', ambón 'drizzle', lindól
'earthquake', bagyó 'storm', bahá' 'flood', etc.

Umuulan.	It's raining.
Umuulan nang malakas.	It's raining hard.
Umuulan sa bundok.	It's raining in the mountains.

Other verbs that belong to this class are the
following.

Lumilindol.	There is an earthquake now.
Umaaraw.	The sun is shining.
Bumabagyo.	There is a storm now.
Bumabaha'.	There is a flood now.
Umaambon.	It's drizzling now.

These verbs inflect for aspect.

Completed:	Lumindól.	There was an earthquake.
Contemplated:	Lilindól.	There will be an earth-quake.
Incompleted:	Lumilindól.	There is an earthquake now.

Ma- adjectives referring to natural phenomena such
as dilím 'darkness', gináw 'cold', ínit 'heat',
liwánag 'brightness or light', etc. occur in topicless

sentences. They are followed by adverbial or locative complements.

Madilim sa bahay.	It's dark in the house.
Maginaw sa Amerika.	It's cold in America.
Mainit ngayon.	It's hot now.
Maliwanag sa banda roon.	It's bright over there.

3. Temporal Sentence

Temporal sentences occur with nouns indicating time or seasonal events followed by adverbs of time.

Bukas na.	Tomorrow, instead.
Lunes kahapon.	It was Monday yesterday.
Mayo sa susunod na buwan.	It's May next month.
Pasko sa Disiyembre.	Christmas is in December.
Todo los Santos ngayon.	It's All Saints' Day today.

4. Sentences with Pseudo-Verbs (Modals)

Gusto sentences are usually topicless when followed by actor focus verbs. The pseudo-verbs have already been discussed in these notes.

5. Sentences with Ka- Verbs

Ka- marks a recently completed action of the verb. Like the rest of the sentences in this section, it has no topic. It is often followed by the adverbial particle lang. The recently completed aspect is formed by the affix ka- followed by the reduplicated CV-/V of the verb base. The reduplication signals action started.

Kakakain ko lang ng almusal.

Kaaaral lang niya ng leksyon.

Kapapasyal lang ni Laura sa Luneta.

Kalalaro lang ng mga bata ng piko'.

Kararating lang nito sa bahay.

Note that since the ka- verb does not take any of the
verbal focus affixes, none of the complements are
focused. Note, too, that lang follows the mono-syllabic
pronouns ko and mo instead of preceding them as with
the other pronouns and phrases.

IX.   EXCLAMATORY SENTENCES

The exclamatory sentences can be classified into
two kinds: one which is a non-comment-topic type of
sentence and the other introduced by interjections.

The non-comment-topic type of exclamatory sentence
is introduced by ang, kay, or napaka-.

Ang is followed by word bases which are the
obligatory elements of these sentences followed by
optional complements.

Ang ganda ng babae!	How beautiful is the woman!
Ang bastos ng lalake!	How rude is the man!
Ang laki ng bahay!	How large is the house!

Adjectives are the most common word bases in this
construction but verb bases can also occur.

Ang takot ko sa iyo!	I was frightened by you!

Like in the ang sentences, kay is followed by
word bases, usually adjectives.

Kay buti nila (sa akin)!	How good they are to me!
Kay ganda ng tanawin!	How beautiful is the scenery!

The complements are usually obligatory in the kay
sentences.

Like ang and kay sentences, the prefix napaka- is

followed by word bases, usually adjectives, and signals
an exclamatory sentence.

Napakatapang niya!	How brave he is!
Napakaduwag ng sundalo!	How cowardly is the soldier.
Napakabait ni Pedro!	How good Pedro is!
Napakatanga nito!	How stupid this one is!

The napaka- sentences like kay sentences usually have
obligatory complements.

The ang, kay, and napaka- exclamatory sentences
can be pluralized by reduplicating the first syllable
of the adjective base.

Ang sentences

Ang gaganda (ng (mga) babae)!

Ang babastos (ng (mga) lalake)!

Ang lalaki (ng (mga) bahay)!

Kay sentences

Kay bubuti nila (sa akin)!

Kay gaganda ng (mga) tanawin!

Napaka- sentences

Napakatatapang nila!

Napakaduduwag ng (mga) sundalo!

Napakababait nina Pedro!

Napakatatanga (ng mga) nito!

Interjections introduce the second type of
exclamatory sentence. The normal comment-topic construction follows the interjection.

Ay, nahulog ang bata!	Oh, the child fell!
Hoy, alis (ka) diyan!	Hey, get away from there!

Sometimes the sentence following the interjection is dropped or a one-word construction, usually a noun or a verb, makes up an exclamatory sentence.

Interjections:	(I)nakapu!	Oh, my God! (lit., Oh Mother!)
	Sus!	Jesus!
	Ay!	Oh!
	Aray!	Ouch!
Nouns:	Sunog!	Fire!
	Magnanakaw!	Thief!
Verbs:	Saklolo!	Help!
	Layas! Sulong!	Go!

X. THE LINKER--A REVIEW

The linker or ligature na is used generally to connect words that are related to each other as a modifier and a modified. Na occurs between the modifier and the modified or vice versa. -Ng is a variant of na which is attached to the first member of the construction when it ends in a vowel or -n. Na occurs after consonants. Na is often omitted in certain constructions but in most instances it replaces -ng in introducing clauses.

1. Some Occurrences of the Linkers

   Before or after the noun head

   Adjective + linker + Noun (or vice versa)

   ang payat na si Maria   the thin Maria
        or
   (si Mariang payat)   Maria who is thin

magandang babae	beautiful woman
<u>or</u>	
(babaing maganda)	woman who is beauti-ful
pulang bulaklak	red flower
<u>or</u>	
(bulaklak na pula)	flower which is red

Demonstrative Pronoun + linker + Noun (or vice versa)

itong bahay	this house
<u>or</u>	
(bahay na ito)	house which is this

Both positions can occur for emphasis.

    itong bahay na ito

<u>Sa</u> Pronoun + linker + Noun

aking bahay	my house
(<u>but</u> bahay ko <u>not</u> bahay na akin)	
iyo-ng bahay	your house
(bahay mo)	

When <u>ng</u> pronouns are used in postposed position the linker is lost. Maybe because of the attributive nature of the <u>ng</u> pronouns, they are never introduced by linkers.

Interrogative Pronoun + linker + Noun

Sino-ng tao ito?	Who is this person?
Aling pagkain ang gustomo?	Which food do you like?
Kaninong lapis ito?	Whose pencil is this?
Ilang selyo ang gusto mo?	How many stamps do you need?
Gaanong monggo ang kailangan mo?	How much mongo (beans) do you need?

Anong kalye ito?	What street is this?

But no linker occurs in the following.

Sino ang taong ito?	Who is this person?
Alin ang pagkain mo?	Which is your food?
Kanino ang lapis na ito?	Whose pencil is this?

Linkers do not occur when noun markers or particles are present.

Some interrogative words are not ligatured, like bakit: Bakit galit ang guro? 'Why is the teacher mad?'

Indefinite Pronoun + linker + Noun

iba-ng tao	other people
sinomang tao	whichever one

Numeral + linker + Noun

Numerals always occur before the nouns they modify.

tatlong babae	three women
apat na babae	four women

Distributive Numerals + linker + Noun

Note that distributives can occur after the noun head but not numerals.

tatlong mamisong mangga	three one-peso-
or	apiece mangoes
(tatlong manggang mamiso)	

Quantifier + linker + Noun

Quantifiers always occur before the nouns they modify. Note that the countable quantifiers (salop, yarda, etc.) are always preceded by numerals with linkers.

kaunti-ng kanin	little rice
marami-ng tao	many people
isa-ng salop na bigas	one ganta of rice
tatlo-ng yarda-ng tela	three yards of cloth
talong pisong isda'	fish worth three pesos

Noun + linker + Noun

batang babae	young girl
kapatid na babae (or babaeng kapatid)	sister

Title + linker + Noun

Binibing Cruz	Miss Cruz
Aling Maria	Mistress Maria
Ginoong Santos	Mr. Santos

Existential Particle + linker + Noun

Affirmative

Mayroong lapis. (but no linker after may)	There is a pencil.

Negative

Walang lapis.	There is no pencil.

Verb + linker + Noun

ang tumatakbong bata or (ang batang tumatakbo)	the running child the child who is running

Adverb + linker + Time noun

tuwi-ng	⎡umaga ⎢hapon ⎣Mayo	every	⎡morning ⎢afternoon ⎣(month of) May

Before verbs

Pseudo-Verb + linker + Infinitive Verb

Gusto-ng kumain ni Maria.	Maria wants to eat.
Ayaw (na) kumain ni Maria.	Maria doesn't want to eat.

Na is often dropped in constructions where it precedes the infinitive form of the verb.

Other pseudo-verbs with linkers.

Maaari-ng ⎤
Kailangang ⎥ magtrabaho si Pedro.
Dapat (na) ⎦

Ma- Modifiers + linker + Infinitive Verb

Matuling lumakad si Pedro.	Pedro walks fast.
Mabilis (na) tumakbo si Pedro.	Pedro runs fast.

Na is often omitted before the infinitive forms of the verbs. Notice however that the linker comes out if some words are inserted between these two elements.

Mabilis bang tumakbo si Pedro?	Does Pedro run fast?

Adverb + linker + Infinitive Verb

Muling kumanta ang artista.	The artist sang again.

Adverb + linker + Incompleted Verb

Laging kumakanta ang dalaga.	The young woman always sings.

Tuwi-ng ⎡umiiyak   Whenever the young
         ⎣nagaalit   woman ⎡cries...
                                 ⎣gets mad...

Before adjectives

Intensifier + linker + Adjective

    Lalo-ng maganda ka   You're more beauti-
     ngayon.   ful today.

Qualifier + linker + Adjective

    Parang   ⎤   ⎡seems   ⎤
    Mukhang   ⎥ tamad si Pedro.   Pedro ⎢looks   ⎥ lazy.
    Masyadong ⎦   ⎣is very ⎦

Adjective + linker + Adjective

    Maganda-ng maganda si   Maria is very
     Maria.   beautiful.

    Tamad na tamad si Pedro.   Pedro is very lazy.

Adverb + linker + Adjective

    Lagi-ng   ⎤   ⎡always⎤
    Talaga-ng ⎥tamad si Pedro.   Pedro is ⎢really⎥ lazy.
    Totoo-ng   ⎦   ⎣truly ⎦

Before adverbs

Intensifier + linker + Adverb

    Tamakbo siya nang lalong   He ran faster.
     mabilis.

In expanded noun phrases, all the modifiers
except mga are linked to the head by the linker.

(Dem) (Pron) (Num)   (Adj)   (Head) (Dem)
Ito-ng ating limang mga maliliit na saging na ito
'These our   five   small   bananas

    (Locative modifier)
na nasa ibabaw ng mesa...
which are on the table...'

    Adjectives in a series, modifying the noun head,
do not have linkers except for the last one following
the conjunction at.

ang maganda, mabait at marunong na estudyante	the beautiful, good, and intelligent student

Two constructions of equal rank are linked together by a ligature when each one is used to identify or clarify the meaning of the other.

ang kapatid ko-ng si Juan	my brother, Juan
sila-ng apat	they, (the) four (of them)
kayo-ng maliliit na bata	you (pl) small children
ang bata-ng kanyang alipin	the child (who is) his slave

Nominalized constructions have linkers connecting the topic to the verb or vice versa.

ang bata-ng tumatakbo sa kalye...	the child running (down) the street...
(or ang tumatakbo-ng bata sa kalye...)	the running child on the street...

Longer modification structures are often linked to the noun head by <u>na</u> even when -<u>ng</u> should have been used.

ang libro $\begin{bmatrix} ng \\ na \end{bmatrix}$ nasa mesa...	the book (which is) on the table...

2.   Some Non-occurrences of Linkers

Linkers do not occur in the following positions.

Before pronouns

Makakapal <u>x</u> itong bagong libro.	The new books (are) thick.
Ano <u>x</u> ito?	What's this?
maliliit <u>x</u> mong anak	your small children

Matanda x ko x siyang kapatid.	She's my elder sister.
anak x kong babae	my daughter
Wala x siyang anak.	He doesn't have a child.
Walang anak x siya.	He doesn't have a child.

Except when what precedes the pronoun is a demonstrative.

Itong ating bahay...	This, our house...
Mahahaba iyang aking bagong lapis.	(Those) my new pencils (are) long.

Before noun markers or particles

Gusto koxng manok. (not Gusto kong ng manok.)	I like chicken.
Anong pangalan mo? (not Anong ang pangalan mo?)	What's your name?

After mga

ang mga x mabubuting tao	the good people

Before the prefix ka- used with adjectives denoting sizes, shapes, etc.

Gaano x kataas ang bundok? (not Gaanong kataas ang bundok?)	How high is the mountain?

Some interrogative words do not have ligatures, like bakit.

Bakit madilim ang bahay?	Why is the house dark?

May, unlike mayroon, is not ligatured.

When one or more words are inserted between two words which are connected by the linker, the ligature is placed after the last of the inserted words.

Note the following examples.

<u>In mayroon/wala sentences</u>

Mayroon/ Wala	(ka)	(pa/na)	(ba)	(Topic)	Linker	Noun	(Topic)
Wala-					-ng	papel.	
Mayroon-					-ng	papel.	
Mayroon/		na-			-ng	papel.	
Wala		pa-			-ng	papel.	
					-ng	papel	si Maria.
					-ng	papel	ang bata.
		pa-			-ng	papel	siya.
		na-			-ng	papel	ito.
				si Maria-	-ng	papel.	
				ang bata-	-ng	papel.	
		na		siya-	-ng	papel.	
		pa		ito-	-ng	papel.	
			ba-		-ng	papel?	
		pa	ba-		-ng	papel?	
		na	ba-		-ng	papel?	
		pa	ba-		-ng	papel	si Maria?
		pa	ba-		-ng	papel	ang bata?
		pa	ba-		-ng	papel	siya?
		pa	ba-		-ng	papel	ito?
		pa	ba	si Maria-	-ng	papel?	
		pa	ba	ang bata-	-ng	papel?	
		pá	ba	siya-	-ng	papel?	
		pa	ba	ito-	-ng	papel?	
	ka-				-ng	papel.	
	ka	pa-			-ng	papel.	
	ka		ba-		-ng	papel?	
	ka	pa	ba-		-ng	papel?	

In gusto/ayaw sentences

Gusto/ Ayaw	(ko/ mo)	(na/ pa)	(ba)	(Ng pron/ phrases)	Linker	Verb	(Ng pron/ phrases)
Ayaw					(na)	kumain	ng bata.
Gusto-					-ng	kumain	ni Maria.
Gusto/					-ng/na	kumain	ng bata.
Ayaw					-ng/na	kumain	ni Maria.
					-ng/na	kumain	niya.
					-ng/na	kumain	nito.
Gusto/				ng bata-	-ng	kumain.	
Ayaw				ni Maria-	-ng	kumain.	
				niya-	-ng	kumain.	
				nito-	-ng	kumain.	
				ko-	-ng	kumain.	
		na-			-ng	kumain	ni Maria.
		pa-			-ng	kumain	niya.
	ko	pa-			-ng	kumain.	
			ba-		-ng	kumain	nito?
			ba	ng bata-	-ng	kumain?	
			ba	ni Maria-	-ng	kumain?	
			ba	niya-	-ng	kumain?	
			ba	nito-	-ng	kumain?	
		pa	ba	niya-	-ng	kumain?	
		na	ba	niya-	-ng	kumain?	
		na	ba-		-ng	kumain	ng bata?
	mo	na	ba-		-ng	kumain?	

In adjectival sentences

Adjective	(ka)	(na/ pa)	(ba)	(Topic)	Linker	Noun	(Topic)
Maganda-					-ng	babae.	
Maganda			ba-		-ng	babae	siya?
			ba-		-ng	babae	si Maria?
			ba	siya-	-ng	babae?	
			ba	si Maria-	-ng	babae?	
		na	ba	ito-	-ng	babae?	
	ka		ba-		-ng	babae?	
	ka	na	ba-		-ng	babae?	

In interrogative sentences

Kanino	(ka)	(ba)	(Topic)	Linker	Noun	(Topic)
Kanino-				-ng	kapatid	si Maria?
Kanino-				-ng	kapatid	ito?
Kanino-				-ng	kapatid	siya?
Kanino			ito-	-ng	kapatid?	
Kanino			siya-	-ng	kapatid?	
Kanino		ba-		-ng	kapatid	si Maria?
Kanino		ba-		-ng	kapatid	ito?
Kanino		ba-		-ng	kapatid	siya?
Kanino		ba	ito-	-ng	kapatid?	
Kanino		ba	siya-	-ng	kapatid?	
Kanino	ka-			-ng	kapatid?	
Kanino	ka	ba-		-ng	kapatid?	